D0754721

RUSSIA

Sakhalin

La Perouse Strait

Occupied by the Soviet Union
in 1945, administered by Russia,
claimed by Japan.

Etorofu-to

Wakkanai

Kunashiri-to
Nemuru-
Strait

Shikotan-to
HABOMAI
ISLANDS

Asahikawa

Sapporo

Kushiro

Hokkaido

Hakodate
Seikan
tunnel

Nakhodka

Tsugaru-
kaikyo

Aomori

Sea of

Japan

Akita

Morioka

NORTH

PACIFIC

OCEAN

Sadoga-
shima

Sendai

Seoul

Ullŭng-do

Liancourt
Rocks

Niigata

Iwaki

SOUTH
KOREA

Kanazawa

Nagano

Utsunomiya

Taegu

OKI-SHOTŌ

Tottori

Gifu

Tokyo

Honshu

Pusan

Kyoto

Nagoya

Yokohama

Tsushima

Okayama

Kobe

Hiroshima

Shizuoka

Cheju-do

Takamatsu

Osaka

Hamamatsu

Kitakyūshū

Matsuyama

Tokushima

Fukuoka

Fukue-shima

Sasebo

Uwajima

Shikoku

Ōita

Nagasaki

Kumamoto

Korea

Strait

N
A
M
P
Ō
-
S
H
O
T
Ō

I
Z
U
-

Kyushu

Kagoshima

Philippine Sea

East
China
Sea

ŌSUMI-SHOTŌ

Sumisu-
jima

Tori-
shima

TOKA
RETT

OKINAWA-
SHOTŌ

AM
SHO

Naha

East
China Sea

124   126   OKINAWA-   128
              SHOTŌ
              Okinawa
              Naha

same scale as
main map

SENKAKU-SHOTŌ

SAKISHIMA-SHOTŌ

RYUKYU ISLANDS

Philippine
Sea

DAITŌ-
SHOTŌ

124   126   128   130

same scale as
main map   142   144

BONIN
ISLANDS

OGASAWARA-SHOTŌ

NORTH
PACIFIC
OCEAN

Philippine
Sea

VOLCANO
ISLANDS

Iwo Jima

142

IMMIGRANTS IN AMERICA

Japanese
AMERICANS

Joanne Mattern

CHELSEA HOUSE
PUBLISHERS
A Haights Cross Communications Company

Philadelphia

Frontispiece: Map of Japan with world map inset. Japanese immigrants braved the harsh journey across the Pacific Ocean to begin a new and better life in the United States.

CHELSEA HOUSE PUBLISHERS

VP, NEW PRODUCT DEVELOPMENT Sally Cheney
DIRECTOR OF PRODUCTION Kim Shinners
CREATIVE MANAGER Takeshi Takahashi
MANUFACTURING MANAGER Diann Grasse

Staff for JAPANESE AMERICANS

ASSISTANT EDITOR Kate Sullivan
PRODUCTION EDITOR Jaimie Winkler
PICTURE RESEARCHER Pat Holl
SERIES DESIGNER Takeshi Takahashi
COVER DESIGNER Takeshi Takahashi
LAYOUT 21st Century Publishing and Communications, Inc.

A Haights Cross Communications Company

http://www.chelseahouse.com

First Printing

1 3 5 7 9 8 6 4 2

Library of Congress Cataloging-in-Publication Data

Mattern, Joanne, 1963–
    Japanese Americans / Joanne Mattern.
        p. cm.—(Immigrants in America (Chelsea House Publishers))
Summary: Looks at the history of Japanese immigration to America, including the reasons for emigration, how Japanese Americans have been treated by American society, and the influence of Japanese culture on America.
Includes bibliographical references and index.
    ISBN 0-7910-7130-8HC   0-7910-7510-9PB
    1. Japanese Americans—Juvenile literature. 2. Japanese Americans—History—Juvenile literature. [1. Japanese Americans. 2. Immigrants. 3. Japan—Emigration and immigration—History. 4. United States—Emigration and immigration—History.] I. Title. II. Series.
E184.J3 M385 2002
973.04'956—dc21

                                                                        2002013475

CONTENTS

INTRODUCTION
A NATION OF NATIONS
Daniel Patrick Moynihan

The Constitution of the United States begins: "We the People of the United States . . ." Yet, as we know, the United States was not then and is not now made up of a single group. It is made up of many peoples. Immigrants and bondsmen from Europe, Asia, the Pacific Islands, Africa, and Central and South America came here or were brought here, and still they come. They forged one nation and made it their own. More than 100 years ago, Walt Whitman expressed this great central fact of America: "Here is not merely a nation, but a teeming Nation of nations."

Although the ingenuity and acts of courage of these immigrants, our ancestors, shaped the North American way of life, we sometimes take their contributions for granted. This fine series, IMMIGRANTS IN AMERICA, examines the experiences and contributions of different immigrant groups and how these contributions determined the future of the United States and Canada.

Immigrants did not abandon their ethnic traditions when they reached the shores of North America. Each ethnic group had its own customs and traditions, and each brought different experiences, accomplishments, skills, values, styles of dress, and tastes in food that lingered long after its arrival. Yet this profusion of differences created a bond among immigrants. Ethnic foods, for example, sometimes became "typically" American, such as frankfurters, pizzas, and tacos.

The United States and Canada are unusual in this respect. Whereas religious and ethnic differences have sparked intolerance throughout the rest of the world, North Americans have struggled to learn how to respect each other's differences and live in harmony.

Our two countries are hardly the only two in which different groups must learn to live together. There is no nation of significant size anywhere in the world that would not be classified as multiethnic. But only in North America are there so *many* different groups, most of them living cheek by jowl with one another.

This is not easy. Look around the world. And it has not always been easy for us. Witness the exclusion of Chinese immigrants, and for practical purposes the Japanese also, in the late nineteenth century. But by the late twentieth century, Chinese and Japanese Americans were the most successful of all the groups recorded by the census. We have had prejudice aplenty, but it has been resisted and recurrently overcome.

The remarkable ability of Americans to live together as one people was seriously threatened by the issue of slavery. Thousands of settlers from the British Isles had arrived in the colonies as indentured servants, agreeing to work for a specified number of years on farms or as apprentices in return for passage to America and room and board. When the first Africans arrived in the then-British colonies during the seventeenth century, some colonists thought that they, too, should be treated as indentured servants. Eventually, the question of whether the Africans should be treated as indentured, like the English, or as slaves who could be owned for life, was considered in a Maryland court. The court's calamitous decree held that blacks were slaves bound to a lifelong servitude, and so also were their children. America went through a time of moral examination and civil war before African slaves and their descendants were finally freed. The principle that all people are created equal had faced its greatest challenge and it survived.

Yet the court ruling that set blacks apart from other races fanned flames of discrimination that burned long after slavery was abolished—and that still flicker today. Indeed, it was about the time of the American Civil War that European theories of evolution were turned to the service of ranking different peoples by their presumed distance from our apelike ancestors!

When the Irish flooded American cities to escape the famine in Ireland, the cartoonists caricatured the typical "Paddy" (a common term for Irish immigrants) as an apelike creature with jutting jaw and sloping forehead.

By the twentieth century, racism and ethnic prejudice had given rise to virulent theories of a Northern European master race. When Adolf Hitler came to power in Germany in 1933, he popularized the notion of an Aryan race. Only a man of the deepest ignorance and evil could have done this. Aryan is a Sanskrit word taken from the ancient language of the civilizations that inhabited the Indus Valley, which now includes Pakistan and much of Northern India. The term "Aryan," which means "noble," was first used by the eminent German linguist Max Müller to denote the Indo-European family of languages. Müller was horrified that anyone could think of it in terms of a race of blond-haired, blue-eyed Teutons. But the Nazis embraced the notion of a master race. Anyone with darker and heavier features was considered inferior. Buttressed by these theories, the German Nazi state from 1933 to 1945 set out to destroy European Jews, along with Poles, Gypsies, Russians, and other groups considered inferior. They nearly succeeded. Millions of these people were murdered.

The tragedies brought on by ethnic and racial intolerance throughout the world demonstrate the importance of North America's efforts to create a society free of prejudice and inequality.

A relatively recent example of the New World's desire to resolve ethnic friction nonviolently is the solution that the Canadians found to a conflict between two ethnic groups. A long-standing dispute as to whether Canadian culture was properly English or properly French resurfaced in the mid-1960s, dividing the peoples of the French-speaking Province of Quebec from those of the English-speaking provinces. Relations grew tense, then bitter, then violent. The Royal Commission on Bilingualism and Biculturalism was established to study the growing crisis and to propose measures to ease the tensions. As a result of the commission's recommendations, all official documents and statements from the national government's capital at Ottawa are now issued in both French and English, and bilingual education is encouraged. But the commissioners recorded that there were many other groups as well.

Toward the end of the nineteenth century in the United States, public figures such as Theodore Roosevelt began speaking about "Americanism," deploring "hyphenated Americans" as persons only partly assimilated—later it would be said insufficiently loyal—to their adopted country. Ethnicity was seen by many as a threat to national cohesion, and even to national security. During World War I, referring to German Americans, Roosevelt would speak of "the Hun within." During World War II, immigrant Germans and Italians were classified as "enemy aliens," and Japanese Americans were settled in detention camps. With time, however, we became more accepting as ethnicity emerged as a *form* of Americanism, celebrated in the annual Columbus Day and Steuben Day parades, the West Indian parade, the Pakistani parade, and in New York City the venerable St. Patrick's Day parade, which dates back before the American Revolution.

In time, the Bureau of the Census took note. In 1980, for the first time, the census questionnaire asked, "What is this person's ancestry?" In parentheses, it stated: "For example: Afro-American, English, French, German" and so on through a list of 16 possibilities, followed by "etc." The results were a bit misleading. Remember, it was a new question. Census officials now speculate that because the first European group listed was English, many respondents simply stopped there. The result was an "overcount." By 2000, however, the bureau was getting better.

The 2000 census also asked people to identify their ancestry. More than 80 percent chose one or more groups from a list of 89 different groups. Most people "specified," as the census states, a "single ancestry," but almost a quarter cited "multiple ancestry." So which is it: are we a melting pot or a "Nation of nations"? The answer is both. Americans share a common citizenship, which is the most important fact of our civic life. But most also feel part of one group or another, especially recent arrivals.

Of which there are many indeed! Since 1970 more than 26 million immigrants have entered the United States; most immigrants have entered legally, but of late not all. For the longest time, anyone could enter. Under the Constitution, drawn up in 1797, even the trade in African slaves was protected for 20 years—a hideous practice, but well established in Southern states. In time, however, hostility toward newcomers appeared, notably tinged with racial fears. In 1882 an act of U.S. Congress excluded further Chinese immigration, responding to pressure from Californians anxious about "cheap labor." Next there was agitation to exclude Japanese, which only ended when the Japanese government, in what was termed a "Gentleman's Agreement," consented to withhold passports from Japanese emigrants. Restrictions on Asians continued until 1965.

Indeed, at the end of the nineteenth century there was much talk about the "Anglo-Saxon race" and its many virtues. The United States had reached an informal alliance with Great Britain, and we were setting up an empire of our own that included the Philippines, Cuba, Puerto Rico, and Hawaii. Weren't we different from those "others"? Not exactly. Migration has been going on across the world from the beginning of time and there is no such thing as a pure race. The humorist Finley Peter Dunne wrote: "An Anglo-Saxon…is a German that's forgot who was his parents." Indeed, following the departure of the Romans from Britain in the year A.D. 410, Germanic tribes, including Saxons from northern Germany and Anglos from southern Denmark, migrated into the British Isles. In time they defined what we now call Britain, driving the Celts to Wales and Ireland, with an essentially Celtic Scotland to the north.

Thus immigrants from the British Isles, approximately a third of the present day population of the United States, were already a heterogeneous group. Perhaps even more importantly, they belonged to many different religious denominations including the Puritan, Congregational, Episcopalian, Quaker, and Catholic churches, and even a small community of Sephardic Jews from Brazil! No group made up a majority; religious toleration came about largely because there seemed to be no alternative.

American immigration policy developed in much this way. Though completely open at the beginning, over time, efforts were made to limit the influx of certain immigrant groups, in the manner of the exclusion of Asians in the late nineteenth century and the Southern Europeans by the early twentieth century. By the 1960s, however, America was already too diverse to pretend otherwise, and immigration was opened to all nations.

The people of North America are the descendants of one of the greatest migrations in history. And that migration is not over. Koreans, Vietnamese, Mexicans, Nicaraguans, Pakistanis, Indians, Arabs, and many others are heading for the shores of North America in large numbers. This mix of cultures shapes every aspect of our lives. To understand ourselves, we must know something about our diverse ethnic ancestry. Nothing so defines the North American nations as the motto on the Great Seal of the United States: *E Pluribus Unum*—Out of Many, One. ■

1 THE JAPANESE IN AMERICA

The story of Japanese immigration is the story of a distinct ethnic group struggling to fit into American society while trying to maintain their own culture and traditions. Because they were a different race from most Americans and because their traditions were so different from the American mainstream, Japanese immigrants could not help but stand out. Although most of them wanted to become part of American society, the Japanese were shunned and discriminated against by the very organizations of which they wanted to become a part.

However, when Japanese immigrants and their families developed their own societies and cultural organizations, they were criticized for not wanting to fit in. As one white newspaper editor wrote in 1913, "The Japanese are intensely distinct and self-conscious as a race and nation. Those who come here, come as

Japanese immigrants, like the farmhands on this Colorado farm in 1942, were hard workers willing to live in harsh conditions. The Japanese have been credited with transforming the landscape of California, where large populations of Japanese first immigrated.

Japanese. They have no thought of becoming Americans." Sadly, it was a no-win situation for the newly arrived Japanese.

OZAWA'S STORY

The clearest example of the struggle faced by Japanese immigrants seeking equality with whites was the fight for citizenship. In 1914, only two classes of Americans were eligible for citizenship: whites and blacks. That year, a young Japanese man named Takao Ozawa filed an application for citizenship. Ozawa had lived in the United States for 20 years and graduated from American schools. Ozawa thought his chances of obtaining citizenship were good, but he was wrong. The court denied his application, even though Ozawa was "in every way eminently qualified under the statutes to become an American citizen." There was just one problem: Ozawa was not white or black.

Ozawa refused to accept the court's decision. He filed an appeal with the United States Supreme Court in 1922. He swore that he was "at heart a true American," but once again, Ozawa was denied citizenship because he did not meet the citizenship eligibility requirement of being either white or black.

Japanese Immigration in Numbers

Japanese Immigration to the United States, 1861–2000, from the U.S. Immigration and Naturalization Service

Decade	Number of Immigrants
1861–1870	186
1871–1880	149
1881–1890	2,270
1891–1900	25,942
1901–1910	129,797
1911–1920	83,837
1921–1930	33,462
1931–1940	1,948
1941–1950	1,555
1951–1960	46,250
1961–1970	38,500
1971–1980	47,900
1981–1990	43,200
1991–2000	67,942
TOTAL	530,186

Despite the discrimination and inequality faced by Ozawa and so many other immigrants, the Japanese became a force to be reckoned with in American society. Between 1860 and 1955, more than 280,000 Japanese came to America. Most of these immigrants arrived in the 30 years between 1891 and 1921.

WHY THEY CAME

Immigrants came from all parts of Japan. Like immigrants from other parts of the world, most left home because of financial hardship and a desire to create a better life for themselves and their children. Many immigrants were younger sons who, by tradition, would not inherit any family property. This limited their ability to make a living. Others sought freedom from Japan's rigid social classes. In America, these people dreamed, they could start a new life, become whatever they wanted to be, and maybe even become wealthy in the process.

THE JAPANESE WORK ETHIC

Despite the discrimination that the Japanese encountered in their newfound home, many sections of American society welcomed the Japanese with open arms. The reason for this was that Japanese provided workers for essential jobs. Between 1900 and 1920—the years of peak immigration from Japan—there was a tremendous demand for farm workers in Hawaii and California. Japanese immigrants were not only willing to work hard and live in substandard conditions, but, in addition, they had a gift for growing fruits and vegetables on even the most barren or swampy land. In 1921, a California official reported that the Japanese had converted barren lands "into productive and profitable fields, orchards and vineyards by the persistence and intelligence of their industry." Three years later, a Japanese farmer described how immigrant labor transformed California. "Much of what you called willow forests then, Japanese took that land, cleared it and made it fine farming land."

Other immigrants traveled to Alaska to work in fish canneries.

Here, they sorted, cleaned, cooked, and canned up to 200 fish a minute. Still more Japanese worked in mines or helped build the railroads that stretched across the western United States.

Women worked just as hard as the men. Many did farm or plantation labor or worked in the canneries. Still more were employed in laundries and shops or as domestic servants.

LITTLE JAPANESE COMMUNITIES

Even as they acquired work, Japanese were looked down on and discriminated against by white society. One way the Japanese coped with these difficult situations was to live together in ethnic communities. Large cities often had neighborhoods that were entirely Japanese. These areas were called names like "Japantown" or "Little Tokyo." "One couldn't believe he was abroad, and one didn't even need to speak English," wrote a man describing the Japanese section of Seattle, Washington, in 1918. Japanese-American writer Harry Kitano explains the importance of cooperation in the Japanese culture:

> One Issei farmer explained to his son that the Japanese in America gained strength by working cooperatively. "If you hold *hashi* [chopsticks] individually," he said, "you can certainly break them all, but if you put them together, why you can't break a bunch of *hashi*. And so, like that, as a family we should stick together, but also as a community we should be sticking together."

GAINING ACCEPTANCE

Children who were born in the United States became much more Americanized than their immigrant parents. They also demanded more acceptance from white society than their immigrant parents had before them. These second-generation sons and daughters would find, however, that society was still not eager to allow "foreigners" to have the same privileges as "real" Americans. Many laws were designed to prevent Japanese

A sign in San Francisco points the way to the city's "Japantown." Like other groups of American immigrants, the Japanese coped with discrimination and the need to preserve their ethnic identity by forming communities with other immigrants from their native country.

and other Asians from becoming fully accepted by American society. Asians could not become citizens or own land. Other laws restricted the number of Japanese immigrants who could legally enter the United States.

Still, the greatest injustice occurred during World War II. Because the United States was at war with Japan, anyone of Japanese origin who lived in the United States—even people who were born in America—was suspected of being a threat to national security. A government order sent all Japanese Americans who lived on the West Coast to internment camps, where they were treated like prisoners and lived behind barbed wire from 1942 to 1945.

Despite the indignities of the internment camps, most Japanese remained fiercely loyal to the United States. This attitude, combined with their hard work and the shame of many white Americans over the internment camps, finally led to a wider acceptance of Japanese in American society. After World War II, laws were changed to allow Japanese immigrants

My America

"As I approached adolescence, I wanted more than anything to be accepted as any other white American. . . . I saw integration into white American society as the only way to overcome the sense of rejection I had experienced in so many areas of my life. . . .

"In high school being different was an even greater hardship than in my younger years. In elementary school one of my teachers had singled out the Japanese-American children in class to point to our uniformly high scholastic achievement. (I always worked hard to get A's.) But in high school, we were singled out by our white peers, not for praise, but for total exclusion from their social functions.

"Once during my college years when friends from Los Angeles came to visit, we decided to go dancing, as we occasionally did at the Los Angeles Palladium. But when we went to a ballroom in Oakland, we were turned away by the woman at the box office who simply said, 'We don't think you people would like the kind of dancing we do here.' That put enough of a damper on our spirits to make us head straight home, too humiliated to go anywhere else to salvage the evening.

"Society caused us to feel ashamed of something that should have made us feel proud. Instead of directing anger at the society that excluded and diminished us, such was the climate of the times, and so low our self-esteem that many of us Nisei tried to reject our own Japaneseness and the Japanese ways of our parents. . . .

"I would be embarrassed when my mother behaved in what seemed to me a non-American way. I would cringe when I was with her as she met a Japanese friend on the street and began a series of bows, speaking all the while in Japanese.

"'Come on, Mama,' I would interrupt, tugging at her sleeve. 'Let's go,' I would urge, trying to terminate the long exchange of amenities. I felt disgraced in public."

The smiling faces of these girls socializing in California's Manzanar Relocation Center during World War II contrast with the grimness of their situation. Seen as threats to national security and forced into internment camps, the Japanese nevertheless remained loyal to the United States.

to become citizens. Gradually, the most obvious forms of discrimination faded away.

Over the past 50 years, American society has become more multiethnic and multicultural. American food, music, art, clothing, and other aspects of life are influenced by traditions from different ethnic groups. Like other immigrant cultures, the influence of the Japanese is prevalent in our everyday life.

2

THE OLD COUNTRY

PHYSICAL FEATURES AND CLIMATE

Japan is located in the Pacific Ocean off the east coast of the continent of Asia. It covers 145,870 square miles, making it about the same size as the state of California. Japan is made up mainly of four large islands: Honshu, Hokkaido, Kyushu, and Shikoku, along with thousands of smaller islands. Japan is surrounded by the Pacific Ocean on the east and south. The Sea of Japan lies to the west, and the Sea of Okhotsk lies to the north.

Mountains and hills cover about 70 percent of Japan. Many of these mountains are covered with thick forests. Most of Japan lies on top of a large undersea mountain range. This part of the earth is unstable, resulting in the formation of many volcanoes and earthquakes. Japan has more than 1,500 earthquakes every year. Although most of these earthquakes are minor, some have

Located on top of an undersea mountain range, Japan's landscape is one of mountains and lush forests. Japan is home to more than 150 volcanoes, and has experienced both earthquakes and tidal waves.

caused tremendous damage and killed many people. Other earthquakes occur underwater and cause huge tidal waves, called *tsunamis*, along the Pacific coast. A tsunami can move as fast as 100 miles per hour, causing tremendous devastation to anything in its path.

There are also more than 150 volcanoes in Japan, including 60 that are active today. Mount Fuji, the highest point in Japan at 12,388 feet, is an inactive volcano. Many Japanese consider this mountain sacred, and thousands of people climb it every year.

Japan's landscape also includes broad, flat plains. Most of Japan's people live on these plains, which provide excellent farmland. Japan's farmland is especially suited for growing rice, which is the country's major crop. Lakes, rivers, and steep waterfalls provide water for crops and drinking.

Most of Japan has a wet, mild climate. There are two rainy seasons. One lasts from mid-June to early July, and the other lasts from September through October. Northern Japan has very cold winters and cool summers, whereas southern Japan has a warm, tropical climate all year long.

Seasonal winds called monsoons help to shape Japan's climate. During the summer, monsoons blow from the southeast and carry warm, humid air from the Pacific Ocean to central and southern Japan. In the winter, monsoons blow from the northwest and bring cold, wet air to northern Japan.

EARLY JAPANESE

Because Japan is an island, it has been able to isolate itself from the rest of the world for much of its history. However, various groups have found their way to the island. Japan's first people migrated there from the Asian continent thousands of years ago. The Ainu were the first to arrive in Japan—about 30,000 years ago. They fished and were hunter-gatherers, who lived in small villages.

Around 300 B.C., a people called the Yayoi came to Japan. Some historians believe that the Yayoi are the ancestors of today's Japanese people. The Yayoi introduced rice farming to Japan.

Over the centuries, Japan was ruled by a series of warlords called emperors. During the 700s, these emperors created a feudal society in which emperors were the supreme rulers. They lived in castles and owned large pieces of land. Peasants swore allegiance to the emperor and lived and worked on his land. Peasants lived in small, simple huts and had few possessions of their own.

Powerful soldiers called samurai protected the emperors. Samurai lived by a strict code of honor and were fiercely loyal to their lord. The leader of the samurai was called the shogun. By 1192, the shoguns had become so powerful that they controlled Japan. The shoguns' rule lasted until 1867.

Under the shoguns, Japan was divided into four classes: samurai, farmers, craftspeople, and traders. Some people such as artists, poets, and priests did not belong to any class. There was also a group called the *eta*, who were considered outcasts. The eta worked in "unclean" jobs such as burying the dead, slaughtering livestock, and tanning animal skins.

The most powerful class in Japan was the samurai. They gave orders, protected the people, and kept the peace. The farmers were the second most important class. Farmers worked very hard to grow rice and other crops and were highly respected. However, because the shogun had the right to take part of the rice crop in exchange for protection, farmers were often left with less than half of their crop to live on or sell to others.

Craftspeople included carpenters, sword-makers, and people who made cloth. The lowest class comprised traders, who bought and sold goods. Traders were not respected as much as craftspeople or farmers because they did not make anything with their own hands. Instead, they earned money from food or items made by other people. Craftspeople and traders lived in small towns or large cities, where there were plenty of customers for their products or services.

Samurai, the powerful soldiers who protected the emperors, came to be the most important class in Japan after the shoguns took control. The samurai gave orders to civilians, protected them from invaders, and kept the peace.

JAPAN'S CLASS SYSTEM

Japan's class system was very rigid. It was almost impossible to leave your class or change your occupation. If a man were a farmer, his son would be a farmer, too. Most people lived and worked in the same place their entire lives. They mistrusted strangers and felt most secure around close family members. An old Japanese proverb advised, "When you see a stranger, regard him as a thief."

Japan's government worked hard to keep the class system in place because it provided a great deal of order and stability to Japanese society. The shoguns worried that foreigners would disrupt the social order that the class system provided. They were especially worried about the influence of Western society from Europe, whose lifestyles and customs were very different from those in Japan. To preserve Japan's independence and traditions, the government passed a law in 1639. This law said that no one from another country could enter Japan, and no Japanese person could leave Japan to visit or live in another country. For the next 214 years, Japan was completely cut off from the rest of the world.

COMMODORE PERRY ARRIVES IN JAPAN

Everything changed in 1853 when Commodore Matthew Perry of the U.S. Navy sailed into Edo Bay. Perry and his crewmen were the first Americans to set foot in Japan. Perry brought a fleet of gunships with him. He demanded that Japan allow foreigners to enter the country and to begin trading with the rest of the world. The Japanese government, fearing the military strength of this stranger, agreed to open its borders to other countries.

The Japanese people were stunned at the arrival of these foreigners and their powerful ships and weapons. Toru Matsumoto, a young man who immigrated to the United States during the 1920s, recalled his grandfather's stories of Perry's arrival. "Perry came in 1853, with four black warships, demanding the opening of the country for trade. The shogun government tottered. Four battleships with guns! Japan possessed only small fishing boats and freight boats."

MEIJI RESTORATION

In 1868, there was a civil war in Japan. A group of warlords overthrew the shoguns and restored the emperor to power. The new emperor took the name "Meiji," which means "enlightened rule." This period became known as the Meiji Restoration.

Emperor Meiji saw how different Japan was from Europe and the United States and decided that Japan needed to be modernized and industrialized to catch up to the rest of the world. Meiji made the army and navy larger and more powerful. He also began building modern factories and industries.

Improving the military and improving industry cost a great deal of money. To raise the money, Meiji levied a tax on the Japanese farmers. Every year, farmers had to pay a certain amount of money based on how much land they owned. If they could not pay, the government took the land away from them. Because prices for rice were very low at this time, many farmers could not produce enough food to pay the taxes. More than 300,000 farmers lost their land. Others lived in extreme poverty. In 1885, one journalist described a common meal eaten by an impoverished farmer: "rice husk or buckwheat chaff ground into powder and the dregs of bean curd mixed with leaves and grass."

Poor living conditions inspired many Japanese to dream of starting a new life in a new land. In 1885, Meiji said that Japanese could immigrate to other countries, and thousands were gripped by "emigration fever." Poor farmers heard that sugar plantations in Hawaii needed workers to harvest the crop. Representatives of these plantations traveled to Japan to hire workers and sign them to three-year contracts. When Japanese men heard that they could make six times more

The position of emperor was restored after the Japanese civil war in 1868. Emperor Meiji, the first emperor to rule after the shoguns, saw the need to industrialize and modernize Japan in order to compete with the West.

Men work in the rice fields of Japan in the late nineteenth century. The broad, flat plains and wet climate of Japan are ideal for growing rice, the country's major crop.

money working in Hawaii than they could in Japan, many quickly signed on as contract laborers.

For most people, life in Japan during the 1800s and 1900s was a constant struggle of hard work and rigid social structures. A person's life was determined by his or her position in society.

This lack of freedom, combined with a willingness to work hard to improve one's lot in life, was a major influence on Japanese emigration.

JAPANESE BEGIN TO EMIGRATE

The idea of saving 400 yen (Japanese currency)—a small fortune in Japan—in just three years was a strong incentive to leave everything behind, even family. Most of the immigrants planned

Working in the Rice Fields

"We made good rice. In our time, in Fukuoka-ken, we would plant rice seedlings one by one along ropes which were set from one end of the field to the other. When we had five people working together, we had five rows being planted at the same time. And the field had to look neat horizontally, vertically, and diagonally. Finishing one line, we went on to the next, after measuring it correctly. When we came to the end of the field, the work was completed.

"After four weeks or so, the seedlings which had looked so fragile would settle more securely in the soil. Then we had to weed. If people did not work hard, the grass grew tall. Since there weren't any chemicals to kill weeds like nowadays, we had to weed by hand and soon lost our fingernails.

"And in those days, we had a horse. We used to spread its dung on thick straw mats, and dry it for manure in the field. We also used human feces. Not now, but in those days, we used it as fertilizer. We would buy and carry it in a cart. We called it *shirimochi: shiri* for 'buttocks' and *mochi* for 'rice cakes.' We took people some rice in return for the manure.

"Then after three to four weeks, the ground got hard, preventing the plants' roots from growing. So we used a coal rake and turned the soil over. And, after about three weeks, we started from the opposite side, making the entire field soft. We used to do this twice and our faces became wet and sticky with mud. . . . And there were leeches, the kind which stick to you and suck your blood. That was the way it was, when I was young."

Osame Nagata Manago,
describing her childhood in Japan in the early 1900s

to live and work in Hawaii for three years. When their contract was up, they would return home with enough money to pay off their families' debts, buy their own land, and start a new and better life.

Immigrating to Hawaii also provided a chance at a future for younger sons in Japanese families. Japan's strict laws of inheritance meant that when a farmer died, all of his land passed to his oldest son. Because the land was not divided among all the children, younger sons had no property of their own. Instead, they had to work for someone else. One man, who later immigrated to the United States, recalled, "I grew up on a farm in Japan. My father owned a fairly large piece of land, but it was heavily mortgaged. I remember how hard we all had to work, and I also remember the hard times. I saw little future in farm work; my older brother would later run the farm." For these young men, there seemed to be little reason to stay in a land where hard work did not bring them as many opportunities as they might find in America.

Emigrating was an opportunity for these younger sons to make enough money to improve their lives. As one young man explained, "I planned to work three years in the United States to save 500 yen and then go back to Japan, because if I had 500 yen in Japan I could marry into a farmer's household, using it for my marriage portion."

Sometimes, people went to America to earn money to pay off family debts. Asakichi Inouye, the grandfather of U.S. Senator Daniel K. Inouye, left Japan after a fire started in his family's home and destroyed several nearby houses. Inouye, who was the eldest son and was already married and a father, was sent to Hawaii in 1906 to pay back the fines assessed against the family. "My father was in debt, so he sent me to this country to make money," Inouye recalled. "I sacrificed myself for my father for the first ten years in the States. I paid back all his debts. At that time I took it for granted that a child would sacrifice himself for his family, although such a situation is almost inconceivable today." Like many other immigrants in this situation, Inouye planned to go back home after the family debt was paid, but he never returned to Japan.

In 1885, the Japanese government chose 600 Japanese men out of 28,000 applications to go to work in the Hawaiian Islands. These men were the start of a wave of immigration that would change the United States forever, as thousands more followed them to a new life and a new land.

3

THE DIFFICULT JOURNEY

The third class accommodations were crowded with more than 1,600 passengers and there wasn't any bunk in which to rest. I slept spreading my own mat and blanket on the wooden floor in the front hatch where there were no windows and no lights. Overhead a piece of net was hung, and when the boat rolled we clung to the net to keep from being thrown around. Day after day the weather was bad and the sea stormy. The hatch was tightly closed and there was no circulation of air, so we were all tortured by the bad odor. As the boat was small, whenever a high wave hit us, the top deck was submerged and the sound of the propeller grinding in empty space chilled us. The food was second class Nankin rice and salted kelp, with dirty clams preserved by boiling in soy sauce. It was impossible fare which now I wouldn't dare to eat.

Chojiro Kubo, describing conditions on board ship in 1897

Japanese who wanted to enter the United States had to pass medical exams. Officials would examine hopeful immigrants for communicable diseases before the immigrants were allowed to enter the United States.

The journey to America was long and hard, and it became a grim memory for the Japanese people who left their homes during the late 1800s and early 1900s. Many immigrants may have even regretted their decision to leave home as they suffered through crowded and smelly conditions, bad food, and horrible seasickness for weeks on end. At these times, the bright promise of a new life in America seemed very far away.

That bright promise was built on stories of plentiful jobs and generous wages waiting for immigrants in the sugar plantations of Hawaii and the farms and orchards of California and other parts of the western United States.

Many immigrants already had jobs waiting for them in Hawaii, arranged by representatives of the sugar plantation companies. These arrangements were known as contract labor. Although contract labor was illegal in the United States, Hawaii was not part of the United States at that time, so the system was legal.

CHINESE EXCLUSION OPENS DOOR FOR JAPANESE

For many years, Chinese immigrants had come to the United States and Hawaii to work on farms, plantations, and railroads, and in a variety of other industries. However, many Americans disliked and distrusted Chinese workers. They worried that these immigrants would take jobs away from whites and also change America's character. In 1882, Congress responded to these concerns by passing the Chinese Exclusion Act, which banned the immigration of workers from China. This law left plantations and other industries scrambling for workers. "By the end of the 19th century, farmers in California complained that tons of fruit and vegetables were rotting in the fields because there were no workers to pick the crops," Japanese-American author Ronald Takaki wrote in his book, *Issei and Nisei*.

Since the Exclusion Act did not apply to immigrants from Japan, companies turned to that country for a new supply of laborers willing to do the difficult and dirty work. One farmer told the U.S. government, "If we do not have the Japs to do the field labor, we would be in a bad fix, because you know American labor will not go into the fields."

GETTING A PERMIT AND BOOKING PASSAGE

For many years, it was very easy for a Japanese citizen to leave the country for America. Until 1908, all he or she had to do was get a permit from the Japanese government. Only criminals or people who might bring disgrace on Japan were refused this permit.

The only other requirement was that the prospective emigrant pass a health exam to make sure he was fit to work and was not carrying any communicable diseases or parasites. This health exam could be quite thorough. In 1905, about 60 percent of the would-be emigrants leaving from Kobe, Japan, failed the exam and were refused a permit.

Other emigrants used folk remedies to trick the health inspectors. Osame Nagata Manago recalled how she passed a test looking for a common intestinal parasite called hookworms. "A person who'd come back from America, who helped arrange my going to Hawaii, told me to eat a lot of nuts which apparently made it difficult for the microscope to find the worms. So I ate quite a lot of these nuts that my mother roasted for me. And I must have been lucky; I was told there weren't any hookworms, so I passed."

During the 1890s, many Japanese emigrants made arrangements through emigration companies. These companies could be found in the major port cities, such as Yokohama, Kobe, Hiroshima, and Nagasaki. In 1899, there were nine emigration companies in Hiroshima alone.

Steamship companies also made it easy for Japanese emigrants to book passage. Kihachi Hirakawa left Japan in 1890 after his father's business failed. "The chance to go to a foreign country came when both steamship companies . . . lowered the fares from 50 yen to 40 yen and 35 yen to 30 yen and at last . . . to 25 yen only," he wrote. Hirakawa continued:

> The English steamer *Abyssinia* . . . was scheduled to sail at 10 A.M., July 27th, 1890. It was just three days before its departure when I noticed this surprising news so I hastened quickly to the office of the Steamship Company, stated my desire to sail on the *Abyssinia*, but also added that I had no passport, and I could not obtain one in a few days. The officer said that a passport was not necessary, and if I paid my fare I would be accepted.

of thy country's glory or stain the brightness of thy family's records, then [call] me no longer father, I will no more [call] thee my son.

Although many immigrants were young men, Japan also encouraged women and families to emigrate. The government felt that family groups were more stable and less likely to get into trouble. By making women part of immigrant society, Japan hoped to cut down on problems such as drunkenness and rowdiness that often occurred among groups of young male workers. Female immigrants also provided an opportunity for young Japanese men to marry someone from their homeland and culture and start a family in America.

LEAVING FROM PORT

An emigrant's journey to America began at one of Japan's port cities. Most emigrants left from Yokohama, Kobe, or Nagasaki. To reach these cities, people walked or rode in carts. Travel became much easier by the late 1800s, when trains linked Japan's major cities.

Emigrants left Japan with little more than a few changes of clothes and some small personal belongings, such as photographs or religious objects. Many emigrants also carried wicker baskets filled with food for the journey, including noodles, dried fish, and rice. When Inota Tawa left Japan for Portland, Oregon, in 1893, he brought "one wicker trunk into which I put one blanket, two collarless flannel shirts and one small towel. No soap. No toothpaste." Some also bought Western clothes before they left Japan, so they would fit in better when they landed in America.

Emigrants usually arrived in the port cities a few days, or even weeks, before their ships left. Until they left Japan, the travelers stayed in emigrant houses, which were boarding houses set up specifically for travelers. Since the house owners made money by renting rooms, they sometimes tricked the emigrants into staying longer. One man who stayed in an emigrant house in Yokohama recalled how a worker took him for all the medical exams:

> ... but as for the most important thing—he wouldn't let me board. Presumably they were calculating to prolong my stay at the lodging house day by day. I was kept there for three weeks. I spent all my travel money there, and so I went back home, managed to get the necessary money once more, came back to Yokohama and again stayed at an emigrant house.

THE ENDLESS JOURNEY

After the emigrants boarded the ships, they were in for a long, uncomfortable ride. The journey from Japan to Hawaii took about 10 days; and the trip to San Francisco took anywhere from two weeks to a month. Most immigrants traveled in steerage, or third class, which was the cheapest— and least comfortable—section of the ship. The seemingly endless journey across thousands of miles of rocking waves on an overcrowded ship was an experience that provided vivid memories for these emigrants for the rest of their lives.

Recalled Takahashi Korekiyo, who traveled to America in 1867:

> The steerage was dark and filled with a foul odor. . . . A large number of us were crowded into it, and each slept in one of the hammocks tied to four poles in three tiers. About at 8 each morning, we were all cleaned and fumigated by smoking peppers for sanitary reasons. We had to eat our meals out of a large tin can together with Chinese laborers. And steerage passengers were provided with three or four large barrels that were placed on the deck where the paddlewheel was, for their need to ease nature. Straddling over two wooden boards on top of these barrels, one had to obey the calls of nature.

Many passengers were violently seasick. Hanyo Inouye traveled

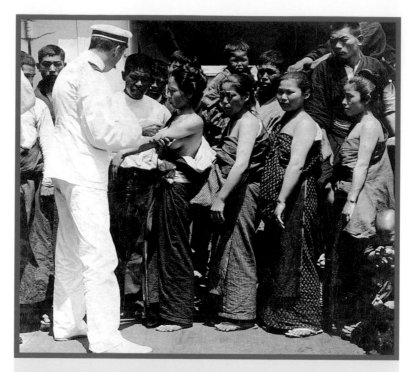

An immigration officer vaccinates Japanese immigrants on a steamship en route to Hawaii in 1904. At the immigration stations located in the Pacific, immigrants underwent medical examinations and had their paperwork reveiwed.

to the United States with her husband in 1923. She wrote:

> I became so awfully seasick that I truly thought I was going to die. A lot of people suffered from severe cases of seasickness all the way. They threw up whatever they had eaten, and because of that they were having a hard time even standing up on their own. I can't forget how much I hated to go to the bathroom, for it was way upstairs. Every time I had to climb up these steep stairs, I tried desperately not to fall off. Oh, it was really scary.

Although they brought their own food and also were served simple meals onboard ship, some immigrants were baffled by Western-style food. One day, a teenager named Chiyokichi Kyono decided to try a Western meal:

> Square slices of bread were served with a yellow lump. I thought it must be some kind of radish pickle, and carelessly I put the yellow lump into my mouth. Ugh! I still remember that

Angel Island

Angel Island opened in 1910. It was called "the Ellis Island of the West" as a reference to the huge immigration station in New York Harbor that processed most of the immigrants traveling to the United States from Europe. However, Angel Island's main function was as a detention center for Chinese and Japanese immigrants, as well as a checkpoint to make sure they were entering the country legally. If a person's papers were not in order, he or she could remain on the island for weeks, months, even years, until the U.S. government decided whether to allow the person in. During that time, the immigrant was held prisoner on the island.

Angel Island included an administration building, separate dormitories for men and women, and a hospital. Living conditions in the dormitories were crowded, with 100 women sometimes sharing a 30- by 30-foot room, sleeping on bunks stacked three high. Inmates had to share toilets, which many described as "dirty." They ate bland meals together in a large mess hall.

For recreation, inmates could walk around the island or play ball in a fenced yard. Women often knitted or read books, while men gambled or played cards. Few visitors were allowed, except for missionaries trying to convert the immigrants to Christianity.

In 1941, the Immigration Service closed Angel Island, and the property was turned over to the U.S. Army. During World War II, the station was used as a processing center for Japanese prisoners of war. After the war, the station was abandoned, and in 1970 it was scheduled to be demolished. However, many immigrants and their children wanted to preserve the station as part of their history. Through the efforts of the Angel Island Immigration Station Historical Advisory Committee, the immigration station was restored and turned into a national historic landmark and a museum.

Wire and mesh enclose female Japanese and Chinese immigrants in a holding room at the Angel Island internment barracks in San Francisco Bay. Angel Island served primarily as an internment location where Chinese and Japanese immigrants could be imprisoned for weeks until they obtained the proper paperwork.

I spontaneously uttered a sound similar to a scream. It was butter, not one bit like a radish pickle! To tell the truth I had never before met up with such a material as "butter." It melted in my mouth, felt sticky, and I couldn't stand the smell.

There was little to do onboard ship. During the day, immigrants could walk around on deck to get some fresh air, but there was nothing to see except the vast expanse of sky and ocean. At night and during stormy weather, passengers stayed below the decks, enduring crowded, hot, and smelly conditions and endless boredom.

The long journey ended with yet another inspection. Immigrants traveling to Hawaii went through an immigration station on Sand Island in Honolulu Bay, and immigrants traveling to the mainland left the ship at Angel Island near San Francisco. At each of these stations, immigrants were given a medical exam and had their paperwork checked by officials. One woman recalled, "The inspector felt our joints at both elbows, around the neck, and on both sides of the groin. Of course it was done while we were fully dressed, but I felt insulted and became furious."

Some immigrants traveled to Canada, where it was easier to pass inspection. There, they slipped across the border and into the United States.

4

HARDSHIPS IN THE NEW HOMELAND

I was amazed at the vastness of the country, there being often more than 100 miles between sizable towns. Because I saw so much land and so few people, I grew uneasy and said, "Why do you waste so much good soil here? Don't you know about the famines and overcrowding in other countries?"

Toru Matsumoto, who traveled from San Francisco to New York City during the 1930s

For Japanese immigrants, as for immigrants coming from other countries, life in America was shocking and not what they expected. Everything—the style of dress, the food, the houses, the working conditions, and especially the language—was different. "Though I had heard about life in America before I left Japan, once I actually landed I was amazed. If I had known more in detail

Many Japanese immigrated to the United States as laborers with three-year contracts. Some immigrants, like the women featured in this picture, worked on Hawaiian sugar cane fields. To escape the harsh conditions in which they labored, many immigrants started their own farms once their contracts ended.

beforehand, I would probably never have come," admitted one female immigrant.

The immigrants' life in America began as soon as they were processed through the immigration station where they landed Once they were free to leave, immigrants departed with family members or friends or simply set off by themselves to find a job and a place to stay.

In the early days of immigration, most of the arrivals were contract laborers, who headed for work on Hawaiian plantations. These immigrants were met by representatives of their new employers. On the U.S. mainland, representatives of farms, mines, and railroads hired many immigrants. These representatives sent the immigrants to camps or other housing near their workplaces.

Living conditions for the Japanese immigrants were primitive. One young man recalled, "Seven of us stayed in one room in the *nagaya* [long house]. At first we spread *goza* [straw mats] on the floor to sleep, then I bought a straw bed for 50 cents at the company store. . . . The purchase was deducted from my pay."

JAPANESE IN HAWAII

Japanese immigrants who came to Hawaii had signed three-year work contracts. The first immigrants found living and working conditions so cruel that they complained to the Japanese government. Japan sent a representative to negotiate better conditions with the labor contractors. However, it took many years before the field workers were treated any better than slaves.

Wrote Chinzen Kinjo of life on a Hawaiian plantation in the early 1900s:

> The life on Ewa Plantation was very hard; getting up at 4 A.M., breakfast at 5, starting to work at 6, and working all day under the blazing sun, . . . we worked like horses, moving mechanically under the whipping hands of the *luna* [overseer]. There was no such thing as human sentiment. At night, instead of a sweet dream of my wife and child left in Okinawa, I was wakened up frightened by the nightmare of being whipped by the *luna*. Because of the perpetual fear of this unbearable whipping, some other workers committed suicide by hanging or jumping in front of the oncoming train.

Even without the cruel treatment, a life cutting sugar cane was incredibly difficult. Workers cut the cane using large knives that blistered their hands. The sharp edges of the leaves and the rough surface of the cane scraped their fingers. The blazing hot sun, humid weather, and the presence of bugs and snakes made the work even more miserable. Haruno Sato, who started working in the sugar cane fields when she was 13 years old, wrote:

> In dressing for work in the sugar cane fields, our biggest worry was to keep out the centipedes and other things from crawling inside. . . . This is how I dressed for work: 1) put on long tight cotton pants. 2) I put on my *tabis* (thick socks) and tightened the drawstring. 3) I firmly wound a *kyahan* (knee to ankle leg wrapping) and tied it to keep the centipedes from crawling between the pants bottom and the *tabis.* 4) I put on my long-sleeved shirt, and 5) I put on my short striped cotton *hakama* (skirt) which was about an inch or two below the knee. 6) I wrapped an *obi* (waistband) firmly around my waist so that nothing could creep in between my shirt and skirt. Sometimes in unwrapping the *obi*, we found centipedes and other insects. 7) I tied on the *te oi* (arm cover which extended from my finger joints to the elbow) to keep bugs out of my sleeves and to prevent the back of the hands from getting cut. I did not wear gloves. 8) I then covered my head with a white muslin cloth, put on my *papale* (hat) and put a pin through the hat to hold everything down. . . . Because we wanted to keep our complexion fair and our faces from being scratched by the sharp leaves, we covered our faces with a man's handkerchief when we worked. Only our eyes were exposed.

Although little could be done to solve the problems of biting insects and the hot sun, working conditions on the plantation eventually improved.

After their three-year contracts were up, many workers refused to sign another agreement to work under such harsh conditions. Instead, they started their own farms. By 1914,

Japanese-owned plantations were producing about 80 percent of Hawaii's coffee beans and 50 percent of its pineapples. Other laborers became carpenters, shop owners, or fishermen, or pursued other trades.

In 1900, Hawaii became a territory of the United States. Because the contract labor system was illegal in the United States, it was also eliminated in Hawaii. Immigrants still worked for the plantations, but now they were free to negotiate their pay, the hours they worked, and the employment conditions. However, plantation owners secretly agreed to keep wages low, so laborers did not have much power.

Japanese workers began to organize into labor unions. Between 1909 and 1919, the Japanese went on strike several times to protest conditions. They demanded higher pay, an eight-hour workday, and better health care. The owners, who had the full support of Hawaii's newspapers, broke most of these strikes. A typical comment came from the *Honolulu Star-Bulletin*, which wrote, "Is control of this industry of Hawaii to remain in the hands of Anglo-Saxons or is it to pass into those alien Japanese agitators?"

JAPANESE WORKERS IN CALIFORNIA

Japanese workers in California did not fare much better than their compatriots in Hawaii. In 1913, California passed a law called the Alien Land Act, which prohibited any Asians from owning land. In 1920, another law prevented Asians from leasing land or living on it as tenant farmers. Because of these laws, most Japanese were forced to become migrant workers. They did all the field work, including planting and harvesting, for low wages, food, and a place to live.

Migrant workers had to travel from place to place, following the growing and harvesting cycles of different crops. As they walked from farm to farm, workers often carried blankets with them to use as bedding. This habit gave Japanese migrant workers a new name: *buranke-katsugi,* or "person who shoulders a blanket."

Conditions were rough, as this description of a Fresno migrant camp during the early 1890s shows:

> During those days around Fresno, laborers did not even carry blankets. They slept in the fields with what they had on. They drank river water brought in by irrigation ditches. When they felt hungry, they devoured fresh grapes. If they ate supper, it consisted of flour dumplings in a soup seasoned with salt. Vegetables were unheard of. Slaving away from 4:00 A.M. to 9:00 P.M., this unhealthy life was intolerable.

Another description, this time from 1900, said:

> The camps are worse than dog and pig pens. They are totally unfit for human beings to sleep in. Rain and moisture seep down from the roofs. Winds blow nightly through all four walls. It's like seeing beggars in Japan living beneath bridges. No one, not even dirt-poor peasants, wants to live in such unpleasant and filthy surroundings. These camps are the reason why so many robust workers become ill and die.

Some Japanese got around the Alien Land Acts by finding a willing white person to buy the land in his own name or by claiming land in their children's names (because children born in the United States were automatically American citizens). I.K. Ishimatsu, a businessman in San Jose, California, recalled the difficulties caused by the Alien Land Acts:

> I don't go so far as to say the alien land laws threatened our livelihood. But if you wanted to lease or own the land for any purpose, you had to use your children's name and if you didn't have your own children, you would have to take a risk and ask someone who was a citizen and hope everything

worked out. A set of books had to be kept up for inspection by the state authorities in order to prove that you were an employee working for a wage. This caused an uneasy feeling because I was informed at the time that the punishment for Alien Land Law violation was condemnation of all the subject's property and imprisonment.

Another Japanese immigrant whose family secretly owned land recalled how fearful she was that they would be found out. "Every day was insecure like this, and whenever we had unfamiliar white visitors, I was scared to death suspecting that they might have come to investigate our land."

PREJUDICE AGAINST THE JAPANESE

No matter where they lived, Japanese immigrants faced many challenges. The biggest of these was discrimination and prejudice from white Americans. Even a rich, successful businessman like George Shima couldn't escape these facts of life. When he bought a house in a wealthy neighborhood of Berkeley, California, neighbors forced him to build a high fence around his house, and newspaper headlines screamed, "Jap Invades Fashionable Quarters."

One of the most outspoken critics of the Japanese was James Phelan, who served as mayor of San Francisco during the early 1900s. Later, Phelan became a United States senator and was instrumental in passing anti-Asian laws. Phelan led protest rallies against the Japanese and made statements such as, "The Japanese are not bona fide citizens. They are not the stuff of which American citizens can be made . . . personally we have nothing against the Japanese, but as they will not assimilate with us and their social life is so different from ours, let them keep at a respectful distance."

Many white residents in California and elsewhere shared Phelan's opinions. These people claimed that Japanese immigrants took jobs away from American workers. They felt that

Japanese Picture Brides

A large number of women came to the United States from Japan to marry as "picture brides." This term came from the fact that the man and woman sent photographs of themselves to each other before they met. As with most marriages in Japanese society, these marriages were arranged.

There was a great demand for Japanese women to travel to America and marry Japanese men who had already settled there. Most Japanese men were not comfortable marrying white American women, and laws and customs made it difficult for such matches to take place. Since it was financially impossible for most immigrants to go back to Japan to find a bride, family members back in Japan arranged marriages, using photographs to introduce the couple to each other. Men did their best to look prosperous and handsome in these photos, often borrowing suits to replace the rough clothes they wore on the plantation and posing with props such as musical instruments.

Many young Japanese women had heard stories about America and were eager to travel there. Becoming a picture bride allowed these women to have an adventure, see a foreign country, and find a husband. "When I told my parents about my desire to go to a foreign land, the story spread throughout the town. From here and there requests for marriage came pouring in just like rain!" recalled picture bride Ai Miyasaki. Another woman explained to her daughter, "I wanted to see foreign countries and besides I had consented to marriage with Papa because I had the dream of seeing America. I wanted to see America and Papa was a way to get there." Other women were simply following the will of their parents, which was an accepted practice in Japanese society.

Picture brides were married before they left Japan. The marriage was part of a Buddhist ceremony conducted between the families of the bride and groom. When the young women entered the United States, they were already legally married, even though they had not met their husbands yet.

Despite the legality of these arranged marriages, many Americans were angry and offended by the influx of Japanese women. These people, exclusionists, wanted to keep American society dominated by the white race. By 1921, pressure from the U.S. government forced Japan to stop allowing females to emigrate. But by that time, there were already 20,000 picture brides in the United States.

Many white Americans feared that the influx of Japanese immigrants would threaten their employment opportunities. This sentiment was especially pronounced in California, which had the greatest population of Japanese Americans in the 1900s.

Japanese-owned stores would charge less for goods and drive white-owned stores out of business. Because Japan was at war with Russia in 1905, some Americans viewed all Japanese as warlike, violent, and untrustworthy.

Most of all, these exclusionists simply felt that Asians were not as good as whites, and therefore did not deserve the same rights and privileges as other Americans. They saw the Japanese as a threat to America itself. During the debate over passage of the Alien Land Act, one white farmer testified:

> Near my home is an eighty-acre tract of as fine land as there is in California. On that tract lives a Japanese. With that Japanese lives a white woman. In that woman's arms is a baby. What is that baby? It isn't Japanese. It isn't white. I'll tell you what that baby is. It is the germ of the mightiest problem that ever faced this state. . . . All about us the Asiatic are gaining a foothold.

Because most Japanese immigrants to the mainland settled in California, that state had the most anti-Japanese feelings. During the first half of the twentieth century, it was not uncommon to see signs such as "Japs: Don't Let the Sun Set on You Here. Keep Moving" or "Japs Keep Moving. This is a White Man's Neighborhood" in California communities.

JAPANESE AND MEXICANS FORM A LABOR UNION

The anti-Japanese movement also hurt Japanese efforts to unionize. Five hundred Japanese and 200 Mexican farm workers formed the Japanese-Mexican Labor Association (JMLA) in 1903. It was the first time in California's history that two different ethnic groups had united in the same labor organization.

For a while, the JMLA was a rare success story. In March 1903, the JMLA led 90 percent of the sugar beet workers in Oxnard, California, on strike. The JMLA announced:

> Many of us have family, were born in the country, and are lawfully seeking to protect the only property that we have— our labor. It is just as necessary for the welfare of the valley that we get a decent living wage, as it is that the machines in the great sugar factory be properly oiled—if the machines stop, the wealth of the valley stops, and likewise if the laborers are not given a decent wage, they too, must stop work and the whole people of this country suffer with them.

The strike worked, and the JMLA became a powerful force in the labor movement. Their success led JMLA's leaders to ask for admission to the American Federation of Labor (AFL), a national union led by Samuel Gompers. However, Gompers would have nothing to do with a union that included Asian members. Although he didn't seem to mind the Mexican members of the union, Gompers told the JMLA, "your union will under no circumstances accept membership of any Chinese or Japanese."

Without the support of the AFL, the JMLA disbanded after a few years. Later, the AFL called for a ban on Japanese immigration, saying that Asian workers "did not share the white workers' God or their hopes, their ambitions, their love of this country."

CONTINUED DISCRIMINATION

Private citizens also took action against the Japanese. In 1905, a group of white Californians formed the Asiatic Exclusion League. Their goal was to use "all possible measures to prevent or minimize the immigration of Asiatics to America." Other organizations, such as the poetically named Native Sons of the Golden West asked questions such as "Would you like your daughter to marry a Japanese? If not, demand that your representative in the legislature vote for segregation of whites and Asiatics in the public schools." This call for segregation would have serious consequences for all Japanese immigrants and their families in the next few years.

LEARNING THE LANGUAGE

Along with facing discrimination and difficult working conditions, Japanese immigrants also struggled to learn English and find a place in American society. At the same time, immigrants also wanted to preserve Japanese traditions. This pull between tradition and adaptation was a

These young girls, wearing traditional Japanese dress in one of California's Japanese parks, exhibit the desire of Japanese immigrants to preserve the traditions and culture of their heritage while making a new home in the United States.

constant conflict, especially as the immigrants' children grew older. In describing his cross-country journey from San Francisco to New York City during the 1930s, Toru Matsumoto writes:

> I didn't understand the conversations of people in buses and subways, and I was miserable to think my English was so poor. If I asked some stranger the way to the post office, he would shout, "That way, and turn right." In such cases, I thought the loud voice was due to anger, not realizing that people thought that foreigners could understand them better if they spoke loudly.

JAPANESE HAIKU

Many immigrants expressed their feelings through *haiku*, a traditional style of Japanese poetry. Although haiku only had 17 syllables spread over three lines, these short poems were eloquent in their despair and disappointment:

> *Issei's common past—*
> *Gritting of one's teeth*
> *Against exclusion.*

> *Hope for my children*
> *Helps me endure much from it,*
> *This alien land.*

AMERICA AS HOME

Despite all their difficulties, the Japanese felt they were part of American society. As the years went by, and their lives in Japan became a thing of the past, immigrants and their children began thinking of themselves as Americans. In 1920, George Shima, the successful potato farmer and president of the Japanese Association of America, explained, "We have cast our lot with California. We are drifting farther and farther away from the traditions and ideas of our native country. Our sons and daughters do not know them at all. They do not care to know them. They regard America as their home."

5 PRISONERS IN THEIR OWN LAND

The house we lived in was nothing more than a shack, a barracks with single plank walls and rough wooden floors, like the cheapest kind of migrant workers' housing. The people around us were hardworking, boisterous, a little proud of their nickname, yo-go-re, which meant literally uncouth one, or roughneck. . . . They would swagger and pick on outsiders and persecute anyone who didn't speak as they did. That was what made my own time there so hateful. I had never spoken anything but English, and the other kids in the second grade despised me for it.

Jeanne Wakatsuki, recalling her days in
a Japanese community on Terminal Island

LITTLE TOKYOS

L ike many other immigrant groups before them, the Japanese tended to settle together. These communities were often called "Japantowns" or "Little Tokyos." Living in a community made up exclusively of members of their own ethnic group allowed the Japanese to hold on to their traditions and gave them a sense of community. Japantowns included

Japanese immigrants typically took hard labor jobs on railroads and farms, and in mines, factories, and the fishing industry. Immigrants typically found themselves in jobs that required working long hours in brutal conditions.

everything an immigrant might need such as stores, barbers, churches, community centers, restaurants, hotels, and professional organizations.

In cities, many Japanese lived in tiny houses or crowded apartment buildings. Conditions were often rough. Immigrant Washizu Bunzo described a Japanese neighborhood in San Francisco during the 1890s.

> This entire area was a San Francisco slum. . . . All the houses were so small and dirty that one could not use them to store things now. . . . When I arrived in America, we didn't need addresses to visit Japanese homes. As long as we were told of such-and-such intersecting streets, we always found the houses. We had only to look for basements with sooty curtains to find them. There we invariably found Japanese living in cave-like dwellings. . . . the kitchens were filthy and disorderly to the extreme. There were no stoves. . . . All cooking was done on one- or two-burner oil stoves. We brewed coffee, toasted bread, and grilled smoked salmon on these oil stoves. Thick, black smoke darkened the rooms, and we were oblivious to the odor which assailed our nostrils.

SOCIAL GROUPS AND SPORTS GROUPS

In Hawaii, communities flourished on and around the plantations where Japanese immigrants worked. Usaburo Katamoto first came to Hawaii as a child in 1896. Later, he returned to Japan, married, and came back to Hawaii with his wife in 1920. The Katamotos lived in a rented house in Kakaako, a large Japanese community in Honolulu. Katamoto recalled years later:

> The owner of the house made it for two family to live. My wife and I had three rooms—kitchen-dining room, living room and a very small bedroom. At first, we had only kerosene lamp, but later on we had electric light. We had to buy a bed because

I did very hard work and couldn't get used to sleeping on the floor. The bed just fit in the bedroom. Toilet was inside the house, because we had sewer system in the area. And we took showers in a semi-public place.

Japantowns and Little Tokyos were also full of community activities and places to socialize. Many Japanese belonged to *kenjinkai,* which were social groups based on the part of Japan where the immigrants came from. Kenjinkai sponsored social activities, but were also a vital source of information about job openings and housing opportunities. In addition, members often lent money to other members, enabling them to buy land or start businesses.

A Japanese man living in Hawaii recalled how nine clubs for immigrants from Okinawa, Japan, joined together to create a large social organization called the *Rengo-Kai.* "At that time there were about 2,000 Okinawans living on Kauai [Hawaii] and over 1,000 were members. . . . We had *ji no tenrankai* (calligraphy exhibition) and *onago no shugei no tenrankai* (women's embroidery exhibition). . . . New Year's parties were very popular."

Japanese communities also had their own sports teams. Baseball was especially popular, and there were organized Japanese baseball teams in Hawaii as early as the nineteenth century. Teenagers had their own clubs, and young people attended dances at Japanese-run halls and hotels. Churches were also an important part of the community's social and cultural life.

THE WORK THEY DID

Work was also an important element in the lives of Japanese immigrants and their families. While many worked on farms or plantations, others found jobs in mines and railroads. Like farm workers, these laborers also faced backbreaking work and rough conditions. Railroad workers were especially troubled by the weather, since they might work in the hot desert or in wind-whipped, snowy mountain ranges. One song describes the hard work and determination of the Japanese workers:

A railroad worker—
That's me!
I am great.
Yes, I am a railroad worker.
Complaining:
"It is too hot!"
"It is too cold!"
"It rains too often!"
"It snows too much!"
They all ran off.
I alone remained.
I am a railroad worker!

Japanese also worked in businesses such as stores, laundries, and restaurants. These jobs could be just as exhausting and time-consuming as farm work. One Japanese restaurant worker recalled getting up at four o'clock in the morning to start the fire in the restaurant stove. "I began to serve guests at 6 A.M. At 11 A.M. when the chief cook prepared dinner, I was in charge of the pantry and arranged the salad orders. My work was finished at 8 P.M."

Factories also provided jobs for Japanese immigrants. Sueko Nakagawa recalled the hard work and unpleasant conditions that she faced when she and her husband arrived in the United States in 1924:

In the daytime I was to work at Alaska Junk Company where my mother-in-law was working. This was the biggest of the junk companies, dealing in old iron, burlap sacks, used clothes and rags, and old newspapers and magazines. I was put in the old magazine and newspaper section. It was a big wooden building three stories high and the junk was piled up to the ceiling on every floor. The dusty smell filled the building. More than twenty Japanese men and women were working there. . . . Since there was no heater during the winter, we had to put on so many sweaters that if we happened to tumble over, we couldn't get up without help. Once entering the room, we felt the dust irritate our nose, and during summertime swarms of fleas swarmed up our legs.

Women worked just as hard, if not harder, than the men. Wives, mothers, and sisters worked right alongside male family members on farms and plantations. A 1915 report on the Japanese in California noted: "Nearly all of these tenant farmers are married and have their families with them. The wives do much work in the field." Women also put in hours of work in family-owned businesses. One woman from Washington State recalled:

My husband was running the Rainier Laundry. At noon I had to prepare a meal for twelve. The employees worked from 8 A.M. to 5 P.M., but I began to fix the dinner at 5 P.M., cooking for five or six persons, and then after that I started my night work. The difficult ironing and pressing was left for me. . . . Frequently I had to work till twelve or one o'clock. Not only I, but all the ladies engaged in the laundry business had the same duties.

Other Japanese women worked for wealthy white families. Their jobs included cleaning the house, cooking meals, tending the gardens, and caring for children.

On top of working full-time, women were also responsible for caring for their husbands and children. Traditionally, the father was the head of the household, and his word was law. Akemi Kikumura, the daughter of Japanese immigrants, described her father's position in their family. "Papa would discipline the children, and even instruct Mama on how to prepare various Japanese foods, how to wear a kimono, how to walk like a refined lady, or how to iron a shirt. The daughters recalled that 'Everything we heard, knew, felt, or dreamed of came from within the household.' Papa forbade his daughters to date, or to engage in any social activity that did not include the family. Even the choice of marriage partners was up to his discretion. He lectured each night during dinner on every subject imaginable while everyone listened in silence. Most of the lectures pertained to some aspect of Japanese traditions, values, or etiquette."

Children were considered precious gifts and were treasured within the family. The first son held an especially honored position, because he was responsible for carrying on the family name. In addition, the oldest son was responsible for caring for his parents when they became too old or sick to work.

JAPANESE EDUCATIONAL VALUES

Although some Japanese children worked alongside their parents, their primary responsibility was to go to school. Japanese immigrants put a great value on education. *Issei,* or first-generation immigrants, knew that there was little chance for them to become accepted in America. They wanted their children to have a better and easier life and put all their hopes for the future on them. Getting a good education was seen as a vital step in this bright future.

One man who benefited from a good education was George Ariyoshi. Ariyoshi was born in Hawaii in 1926 and became the first Japanese-American governor in the United States when he was elected governor of Hawaii in 1973. Ariyoshi credited his success to his father's attitudes toward education:

> Early on, my father encouraged me to attain a good education. He once told me that one can earn a fortune but that can be lost as well. An education, however, can never be taken away. When I was an eighth grader, I told my father I wanted to become a lawyer. He was very pleased and told me he would

Tracing Your Roots

If you are of Japanese descent, there are a variety of resources to help you research and record your family history. Begin in the present and work into the past, taking accurate and organized notes while you research. Although the names of your ancestors are the most important record on the family tree you will create, it is necessary to add details to distinguish your family members from others. Detailed records are organized by family groups, sets of parents, and their children. This includes birth, marriage, and death dates and their locations for each person. It is possible to print blank charts from genealogy research websites, or you can use free online or downloadable genealogy record programs instead.

Start from your memory, listing yourself, your parents, and your siblings on your blank family group record. Many records such as census, land titles, and birth, marriage, and death certificates list information by county as well as city. Always include county information as you compile your records. Then begin a new family group record for each of your parents, listing their siblings and their parents. Once you have listed as much information as you can remember, ask your relatives to fill in any blanks. It is easiest to work on one family line at a time, such as your maternal grandfather's family.

Your living relatives are a valuable source of information. Their memories and stories are a meaningful part of your family tree. They also will have a great deal of information recorded in family bibles, diaries, letters, photographs, birth certificates, marriage licenses, deeds, wills, and obituary clippings. As you fill in your record, list whether the source of information was a letter, a conversation with your grandmother, or information off your great-uncle's military discharge papers that were stored in the attic. This will make it easier to verify your information.

Local history centers and genealogy societies specialize in assisting people in compiling records and have searchable data such as microfilm census records. Your local library also has many resources. The Internet has made it easy to research your family from home, and there are hundreds of websites for genealogists to access particular information. Many sites allow researchers documenting the same family lines to share their files with another. It is always important to double-check the sources others used to find their information so that you can be sure that your ancestors are truly the same.

give up everything, even the shirt off his back, in order to make my hopes possible. That guidance and my parent's generous support have been very much responsible for my educational advancement and whatever measure of success I have been able to attain.

FIGHTING SEGREGATION

Although many immigrants sent their children to Japanese schools so they would retain their traditions and behavior, other children attended American schools. For many children living in Japantowns, school was one of the first places they were integrated with whites. However, they soon learned that integration did not mean equality. "The Mexican and Japanese children were usually seated at the back of the classroom," recalled Mary Nagao, who was born in San Bernardino, California, in 1920:

> If the new textbooks ran out as they were being passed out, we got the older ones. We were always last in the cafeteria food line. . . . So although no one was physically abusive, there was that quiet snobbery. "You stay in your place and we'll leave you alone." It started in the lower grades and you learned to work around it.

Another *Nisei,* or child of Japanese immigrants, recalled the segregated society of Oakland, California, in 1924: "We played with neighborhood kids, so there was a mixed group. But as we got older, it was a little different. We were very friendly with them at school, but our social life was separate. I remember in high school there was a Hi-Y—it's like a teenage senior-high club. It was segregated, all Japanese-American."

Some city officials wanted to make that segregation legal. On October 11, 1906, the San Francisco school board announced that all Asian students would have to go to a separate school. School principals were told to send "all Chinese, Japanese and Korean children to the Oriental School."

When the Japanese government heard about the segregation order, it was furious. Japan sent a protest to Washington D.C., claiming that the decision violated a treaty guaranteeing equal educational opportunities to Japanese children. The incident soon escalated into an international crisis.

U.S. President Theodore Roosevelt respected Japan because of its military power. He did not want the issue to make enemies of the two countries. Roosevelt told the San Francisco Board of Education to cancel the segregation order. "The cry against them [the Japanese] is simply nonsense," Roosevelt wrote. Roosevelt met with San Francisco's mayor and the school board and worked out a deal. The city's Japanese students would be allowed to attend public school, and Roosevelt would negotiate with Japan to reduce the number of immigrants coming to the United States. This compromise led to the Gentlemen's Agreement of 1908, which stopped the immigration of Japanese laborers.

JAPANESE AMERICAN CITIZENS LEAGUE

As the children of Japanese immigrants grew older, sharp differences began to appear between them and their immigrant parents. While the Issei were willing to remain on the fringes of American society, endure tremendous hardships, and take on jobs that whites were unwilling to do, the Nisei felt they were true Americans, who deserved to be treated equally.

During the 1930s, many Nisei organized Japanese American Democratic clubs to fight against racism and unfair laws. Organizations such as the American Loyalty League in San Francisco, and Seattle's Progressive Citizens' League, were formed to promote the welfare of Japanese Americans and show they were good citizens.

The most important of these organizations was the Japanese American Citizens League (JACL), a national organization founded in Seattle, Washington, in 1930. One of the JACL's leaders was James Sakamoto, editor of the *Japanese American Courier.* Sakamoto felt that the Nisei should not think of themselves as Japanese, or even Japanese Americans. They should become "one hundred percent Americans."

Sakamoto set three goals for the JACL: "contributing to the social life of the nation, living with other citizens in a common community of interests and activities to promote the national welfare; contributing to the economic welfare of the nation by taking key roles in agriculture, industry, and commerce; and contributing to the civil welfare as intelligent voters and public-spirited citizens."

Sakamoto also urged members to achieve their goals through enterprise and hard work, not violence. "Agitation begets agitation, and this can never lead to the best results." Instead, he counseled, JACL members should work on self-improvement and achieving success in the business community.

The JACL sponsored many political and social events. One member of the League during the 1930s recalled, "Between wienie bakes and the beaches and dances, *Nisei* would gather at church and JACL meetings to ponder ways of getting out the *Nisei* vote, planning ways of putting up Japanese American candidates for political offices, mixing more into the larger American community, talking about the future of Japanese churches and citizenship for the *Issei.*" Most of all, the JACL encouraged the Nisei to be patriotic. Sakamoto wrote:

> Only if the second generation as a whole works to inculcate in all its members the true spirit of American patriotism can the group escape the unhappy fate of being a clan apart from the rest of American life. Instead of worrying about anti-Japanese activity or legislation, we must exert our efforts to building the abilities and character of the second generation so they will become loyal and useful citizens who, some day, will make their contributions to the greatness of American life.

Between 1930 and 1940, the JACL grew from 8 to 50 chapters

and had more than 5,600 dues-paying members. The League is still active today, promoting the rights and responsibilities of Japanese Americans, and honoring their contributions to American society.

AMERICAN CITIZENSHIP DENIED

It was clear to most Japanese Americans that the best way to win acceptance and equality with whites was to become American citizens. However, a 1790 law barred Japanese from becoming citizens because they were not white. The issue of citizenship led to a fierce debate between whites and Japanese. Many whites agreed with a newspaper editor who wrote in 1913, "The Japanese are intensely distinct and self-conscious as a race and a nation. Those who come here, come as Japanese. They have no thought of becoming Americans."

On the other hand, a Japanese journalist wrote, "Open the doors of citizenship to them, encourage them to become worthy members of the commonwealth, and their hearts will glow with hope and they will strive to prove their right and fitness to become American citizens."

In 1922, Takao Ozawa took his fight for American citizenship all the way to the Supreme Court. Takao argued that Asians were not specifically denied citizenship by law, so that he should be eligible. However, the Supreme Court disagreed, saying that, "even though the lawmakers had failed to *exclude* the yellow races of Asia, it would be necessary to name them in addition to the free white persons if they were to be *included* among the favored."

Japanese Americans were bitterly disappointed by this decision. The community's feelings were expressed by a Japanese newspaper, which wrote, "The slim hope that we had entertained . . . has been shattered completely."

Despite the setback regarding citizenship, Japanese Americans were beginning to win respect from American society by the late 1930s. Of course, there were still many exclusionists and racists who felt the Japanese did not belong in America. However, the immigrants and their children's hard work and social responsibility were beginning to pay off. Then came Pearl Harbor, and the darkest chapter in Japanese American history.

WORLD WAR II AND INTERNMENT CAMPS

On December 7, 1941, during World War II, Japan attacked the Pacific Fleet at Pearl Harbor, a U.S. military base in Hawaii. The attack killed or wounded approximately 3,000 U.S. naval and military personnel, and destroyed a large number of American ships. The next day, President Franklin Roosevelt declared war on Japan. Suddenly, Japanese Americans were a dangerous enemy.

Japanese Americans were stunned to be at war. Frank Chuman, a student at the University of California at Los Angeles School of Law, recalled the nervousness that swept the community: "Later, I drove to Japanese town [in Los Angeles], to see what was going on. It was like a ghost town. I felt very conscious of the fact that I had a Japanese face. I wondered how we would be treated by our non-Japanese friends and neighbors. I felt very much alone, silently hoping for some words of comfort but fearing that my features would cause me to be the target of hatred and suspicion for what the Japanese navy had done."

Immediately after the attack, the FBI arrested almost 2,200 members of the Japanese community, including many community activists, claiming they were a threat to national security. The public also viewed the Japanese as enemy agents and spies who might aid Japan in attacking or even occupying the United States. Many political groups and newspapers called for all residents of Japanese ancestry to be removed from the West Coast.

On February 19, 1942, President Roosevelt signed an order that removed 110,000 Japanese—including 70,000 Nisei who were American citizens—from their homes in California, Oregon, and Washington. They would be moved

On December 7, 1941, Japanese submarines and carrier-based planes attacked the U.S. Pacific Fleet at Pearl Harbor, Hawaii, killing or wounding approximately 3,000 naval and military personnel. This attack pulled the United States into World War II and began a period of extreme anti-Japanese sentiment in the United States.

to internment camps throughout the United States until World War II was over.

Despite the unfairness of the act and the disruption it caused, most Japanese followed orders. As instructed, they showed up at reporting centers and boarded trains to the camps. There they faced a prison-like existence. The camps were surrounded by barbed wire and patrolled by armed guards. Families lived in barracks or converted horse stables, and meals were served in large mess halls.

In this picture, Japanese Americans board trains headed for California's Manzanar Relocation Center. Then U.S. President, Franklin Delano Roosevelt, ordered the Japanese into internment camps.

One detainee, Ted Nakashima, described the difficult life in the internment camps:

> The guards are ordered to shoot anyone who approaches within twenty feet of the fences. . . . The food and sanitation problems are the worst. . . . Dirty unwiped dishes, greasy silver, a starch diet, no butter, no milk, bawling kids, mud, wet mud that stinks when it dries, no vegetables. . . . Can this be the same America we left a few weeks ago?

One of the most well known internment camps was Manzanar, California. As with other camps, the detainees did their best to live a normal life, despite the strange circumstances.

Jeanne Wakatsuki recalled, "As the months at Manzanar turned to years, it became a world unto itself, with its own logic and familiar ways. . . . In most ways it was a totally equipped American small town, complete with school, churches, Boy Scouts, beauty parlors, neighborhood gossip, fire and police departments, glee clubs, softball leagues, Abbott and Costello movies, tennis courts, and traveling shows."

Another detainee provided a similar description of life at Manzanar.

> In some way, I suppose, my life was not too different from a lot of kids in America between the years 1942 and 1945. I spent a good part of my time playing with my brothers and friends, learned to shoot marbles, watched sandlot baseball and envied the older kids who wore Boy Scout uniforms. We shared with the rest of America the same movies, screen heroes and listened to the same heartrending songs of the forties. We imported much of America into the camps because, after all, we were Americans.

JAPANESE AMERICANS IN THE ARMY

Ironically, while their families were interned, many Nisei joined the army to fight for America. In 1943, President Roosevelt created the 442d Regimental Combat Team specifically for Japanese-American soldiers. Young men accepted to the 442d were thrilled. "Grown men leaped with joy on learning that they were finally going to be given the chance on the field of battle to prove their loyalty to the land of their birth," recalled Spark Matsunaga, a member of the 442d who went on to become a U.S. senator from Hawaii. The 442d Regiment served bravely in Europe and the Pacific, winning more than 3,600 Purple Hearts, 810 Bronze Stars, 342 Silver Stars, 47 Distinguished Service Crosses, and 6 distinguished unit citations. The 442d won more military honors than any other unit in American military history.

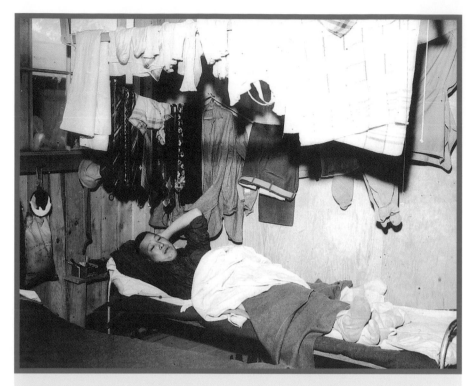

A man sleeps in the small barracks of one of the most well-known relocation camps in Manzanar, California. It would not be until a Supreme Court ruling in 1944 that the Japanese would be able to leave the camps.

CLOSING OF INTERNMENT CAMPS

Meanwhile, back in America, several Japanese Americans filed lawsuits against the government, saying that their removal from their homes and internment in the camps were illegal. In December 1944, the U.S. Supreme Court agreed. The court said that the government had no right to restrict the freedoms of U.S. citizens, no matter what their ethnic background was. The court also said that the racism that led to the creation of the camps "bears no reasonable relation to military necessity and is utterly foreign to the ideals and traditions of the American people." Over the next few months, the camps closed, and thousands of Japanese Americans went back home.

Although some returning Japanese were able to pick up the pieces of their lives, many had lost everything—their houses, land, possessions, and jobs. "I went back in '45 [to Washington] to see what was left of my property, and everything was gone," one man recalled. "What I had left with the man who I thought was a friend, had known for a long time, all my adult life, he wasn't there, and all the stuff I left there in his care [was now owned by another family]. This man shows me a government bill of sale for all the stuff I left . . . farm equipment, tools, household goods . . . so I had nothing to go back to." Many detainees settled in new places, spreading into other parts of the United States away from the West Coast.

In 1988, the United States government formally apologized to all the survivors of the World War II internment camps. In addition, Congress voted to pay each survivor $20,000 in reparations. The checks were mailed with a letter from President George Bush, stating in part: "A monetary sum and words alone cannot restore lost years or erase painful memories; neither can they fully convey our Nation's resolve to rectify injustice and to uphold the rights of individuals. We can never fully right the wrongs of the past. But we can take a clear stand for justice and recognize that serious injustices were done to Japanese Americans during World War II."

The place of the Japanese in American society would never be the same.

CHAPTER

6

THE BARRIERS ERODE

ACCEPTANCE OF THE JAPANESE

After World War II ended, the Japanese found themselves more accepted in America. Part of that acceptance came from the hard work and patriotism that the Japanese had shown for so long. Nisei who had attended college were able to get better jobs, breaking down more stereotypes and barriers in society. A general opening-up of society for all ethnic groups during the 1950s and 1960s also helped the Japanese become more integrated and accepted. By the 1970s, Japanese Americans held a significant number of professional and management-level jobs.

The war also changed American perceptions of the Japanese. The bravery shown by members of the 442d Regiment touched many people. During a ceremony presenting the Distinguished

These Japanese-American children, hands over their hearts during the "Pledge of Allegiance," were interned during World War II. After 1945, the Japanese became more accepted in American society, partly due to the patriotism they had long displayed.

Service Cross to the mother of a Japanese man killed in World War II, General Joseph Stilwell said, "The *Nisei* bought an awful big hunk of America with their blood. You're damn right those *Nisei* boys have a place in the American heart, now and forever. . . . We cannot allow a single injury to be done them without defeating the purpose for which we fought."

Another former internee, Yoshiko Uchida, also gave the Nisei soldiers credit for changing American attitudes about the Japanese:

> I left Topaz [an internment camp in Utah] determined to work hard and prove I was as loyal as any other American. . . . I felt I was representing all the Nisei, and it was sometimes an awesome burden to bear. When the war was over, the brilliant record of the highly decorated Nisei combat teams, and favorable comments of the GIs returning from Japan, helped alleviate to some degree the hatred directed against the Japanese Americans during the war.

Other Americans felt tremendous guilt about the wartime internment of the Japanese, many of who were fellow citizens. They were especially shamed to realize how much some Nisei soldiers had sacrificed for their country while their families were detained in internment camps.

A young internee, who later lost a leg fighting with the 442d Regiment in Italy, recalled an episode that illustrated how white American attitudes had changed:

> One of the fellows had a service station and when I first came back, I went into this station. I knew the family. The fellow's father was one of the old settlers in Loomis and knew my father well. When he saw me at the service station getting out, struggling to get out of the car, to fill it with gas, he came out. After I was all through he said, "I'd like to talk to you." I said, "Hop in." He traveled with me down the road from the station. He said, "Y'know I was one [lousy person]. I had signs on my service station saying 'No Jap trade wanted.'" He said, "Now, when I see you come back like that, I feel so small." And he was crying. That was one of my experiences when I came back.

These men of the 442d Combat team were among many Japanese-American soldiers whose demonstrations of courage in World War II helped change the negative perceptions many people had toward Japanese Americans.

LEGAL AND POLITICAL CHANGES

Legal changes also helped the Japanese win a bigger share of the American dream. The year 1952 was one of many important milestones. California repealed the Alien Land Laws, which had prevented Asians from owning land. Now

How Others Saw Them

In a memo to the secretary of war on February 14, 1942, General John L. DeWitt said, "In the war in which we are now engaged racial affinities are not severed by migration. The Japanese race is an enemy race and while many second- and third-generation Japanese born on United States soil, possessed of United States citizenship, have become 'Americanized,' the racial strains are undiluted. . . . It, therefore, follows that along the vital Pacific coast over 112,000 potential enemies, of Japanese extraction, are at large today. There are indications that these are organized and ready for concerted action at a favorable opportunity."

The *Hawaiian Gazette* described how Hawaiians regarded Japanese immigrants in an article printed in June 1868: "At first glance these Japanese looked like good people. They were brimming with vigor and zest. These people from the Empire of Japan did not appear to have visited foreign countries before and strolled through the streets as if they were enjoying the novelty of it all very much. They are of a very polite race. They quickly took to our greeting, 'Aloha!' and repeatedly returned the courtesy with 'Aloha, Aloha.' In spite of their shabby clothing, they did not appear to be timid in the least. On the whole they created a favorable impression and were greeted warmly by white residents and natives alike. It is hoped that they will turn out to be amiable and useful workers."

H.A. Mills, author of *The Japanese Problem in the United States* (1915), described Japanese railroad workers: "The Japanese found favor with the road-masters and foremen because of their efficiency, and their good behavior in camp. On the whole they proved to be better workmen than any other of the immigrant races, the Mexican excepted, and the absence of brawls in camp set them in strong contrast to certain other competing races."

The Los Angeles Times, 1942: "A viper is nonetheless a viper wherever the egg is hatched—so a Japanese American, born of Japanese parents—grows up to be a Japanese, not an American."

A 1905 U.S. government report stated: "Whenever a Japanese is given a position as an assistant to a skilled worker, or in a mechanical position, he becomes a marvel of industry, disregarding hours, working early and late . . . and doing the work which properly belongs to the workman he is assisting."

Japanese, along with Chinese, Koreans, and other Asians, were free to own property in their own names. That same year, the McCarren-Walter Act was passed, allowing Japanese and other Asians to become American citizens. By 1965, 46,000 Issei had received their citizenship papers. The McCarren-Walter Act also allowed some Japanese immigration to the United States, changing a law that had been passed 28 years earlier.

Tremendous changes were also empowering Japanese Americans in Hawaii. Hawaii had been a United States territory since 1900. In 1959, it was finally accepted as the fiftieth state. Because Hawaii had such a large population of Japanese, many of the state's new officials were Japanese. Hawaii became the first U.S. state to elect public officials of Japanese ancestry in large numbers. The most prominent members of this new political class were Daniel K. Inouye and Spark Matsunaga, both sons of Issei. Both were elected as Hawaii's representatives to the United States Senate.

As American society opened up after World War II, Japantowns began to die out. Although major cities in California, Oregon, and Washington still have large Japanese populations, residents have settled in different places as well. Laws prohibiting discrimination in housing have helped Japanese spread into other communities. Scholars Robert Wilson and Bill Hosokawa report that, "gradually, social class rather than ethnicity is influencing residential patterns, Japanese American families live where they can afford to without regard to the presence of their peers."

At the same time, Japanese who moved into other parts of the United States found many areas were more accepting of their presence than California had been. George Sakamoto moved to Seabrook, New Jersey. This was a factory town centered around the Seabrook Frozen Foods Plant, which

On June 21, 2000, President Clinton presented the Medal of Honor to Senator Daniel K. Inouye of Hawaii for his service in World War II. Hawaii became the first state to elect large numbers of individuals of Japanese ancestry to positions in local, state, and national governments.

employed a large number of Japanese. Sakamoto recalled, "It hasn't been bad here. Many Japanese families came here with practically nothing, and now their children are well educated and are doctors and lawyers. The Japanese have done well here. The people in New Jersey were more tolerant and understanding than those in California."

The days of isolation and outright discrimination were over. The Japanese were finally acknowledged as an essential and vital part of America.

7 INTO THE MELTING POT:
The Japanese–American Influence

The status the Japanese Americans have achieved in the United States despite monumental obstacles speaks eloquently of their qualities as people. When their ancestors came east to America, they brought to this nation worthy ingredients to enrich the mosaic of the U.S.A.

Robert Wilson and Bill Hosokawa,
East to America: A History of the
Japanese in the United States

The Japanese are truly an American success story. From humble beginnings, they have become an important part of American society, with an effect on our culture that far outweighs their relatively small presence in our population.

Japanese Americans place a great deal of emphasis on education from an early age. Because of the importance placed on education, a high percentage of Japanese-American men and women complete four-year college degrees.

ASSIMILATION

According to the 2000 U.S. Census, there are 796,700 Japanese Americans in the United States. This is less than 1 percent of the nation's total population. Over the past 20 years, the rate of immigration from Japan has dropped considerably. Today, 75 percent of Japanese Americans were born in America.

The Japanese are considered to be one of the most assimilated of all Asian-American groups. They live and work in many different neighborhoods alongside whites and members of other ethnic and cultural groups. About one-third of all Japanese Americans on the mainland marry non-Japanese. This rate is even higher in Hawaii, where half of all Japanese marry non-Japanese. This intermarriage has helped Japanese assimilate even more into American culture.

Japanese work in all types of jobs. Because education is so important in Japanese culture, they are able to succeed in a number of professional and technical fields. Forty percent of all Japanese-American men and 25 percent of Japanese-American women complete a four-year college degree, which is a higher percentage than any other ethnic group, including whites. The Japanese make up a large part of the workforce in such fields as engineering, computer technology, and business management. Others are doctors, lawyers, or teachers.

Because they are well educated and work in well-paying jobs, Japanese Americans have become part of the middle class and upper-middle class. Many own their own homes and are a vital part of communities. Although large cities, especially on the West Coast of the United States, still have concentrated populations of Japanese Americans, most have spread out into integrated communities around the country. A high percentage of Japanese Americans live in suburban areas, where they are able to buy their own homes and become an active part of the community.

FAMILY TRADITIONS AND IDENTITY

Despite their assimilation into American society, Japanese retain many family and social traditions. Many Japanese parents send their children to Japanese schools on weekends. These schools teach Japanese language, customs, and culture such as music and arts-and-crafts. By doing this, Japanese parents hope to keep their homeland's heritage alive for future generations.

Japanese Americans also want their children to learn about their history. They feel that without a sense of the past, a person cannot know who he or she really is. "You are a homeless dog without your identity," said one Issei. "Though we are U.S. citizens, we are Japanese. . . . Losing identity is the same as losing money; you lose your way of life. . . . I believe children and grandchildren must know the way their grandparents walked."

JAPANESE HOLIDAYS

The Japanese celebrate many special holidays. One of the most important is Oshogatsu, or Japanese New Year, which

In celebration of the Japanese New Year, these women make *mochi*, a traditional food made out of rice, which symbolizes good fortune.

is celebrated on January 1. On New Year's Eve, Japanese eat special noodles called *soba*. Because these noodles are long and thick, they symbolize a long life. On New Year's Day, families get together and share traditional food such as *tai* (Japanese fish) and *mochi* (sweet rice balls that are a symbol of good fortune).

Kelly Hanzawa, who was born in New Jersey after World War II, describes some of her family's New Year's traditions:

The family gets together and has a traditional breakfast. Then the female members of the family stay home and receive gifts from people who visit. My father was always gone with the men, going from house to house to wish the families Happy New Year's. It is a big holiday for Japanese families. Food is prepared for days on end—*mochi*, for example. For breakfast we would have *ozoni*, which is fish broth made with rice cakes. Also a lot of liquor is served. And I still observe this tradition.

Notable Japanese Americans

Jokichi Takamine (1854–1922) After arriving in the United States in 1884, Takamine, a chemist, worked to isolate the hormone adrenalin. He also found the Japanese Association of New York and gave money to help other first-generation Japanese immigrants work in chemistry, art, and music.

Isamu Noguchi (1904–1988) was born in Los Angeles of a Japanese father and American mother. He was greatly influenced by Asian art when he lived in Japan as a child. Noguchi gave up a career in medicine after receiving a Guggenheim Fellowship to study art in 1927. His most famous sculpture, "Red Cube," is on display in New York City.

S.I. Hayakawa (1906–1992) Hayakawa was born in Vancouver, Canada, to Japanese immigrant parents and became a U.S. citizen in 1955. Hayakawa served in the U.S. Senate as a Republican from California and was a respected educator. He is best known for his efforts to promote English as a national language.

Minoru Yamasaki (1912–1986) An architect born in Seattle, Yamasaki's most famous design was New York City's World Trade Center. He designed more than 300 buildings, including Los Angeles's Western Century Plaza Hotel and Tower, the Federal Science Pavilion at Seattle's Century 21 Exposition, and Saudi Arabia's Dhahran Airport.

Daniel Ken Inouye (1924–) The first Japanese American elected to the U.S. House of Representatives and the Senate, Inouye lost his right arm while fighting with the U.S. Army in Europe during World War II. Inouye became a lawyer after being discharged from the army in 1947. When Hawaii became a state in 1959, Inouye was elected its first member of the House of Representatives. In 1963, he was elected to the U.S. Senate.

The Japanese also have special holidays to celebrate children. March 3 is Girls' Day, and May 5 is Boys' Day. On Girls' Day, which is also called Doll's Festival Day, families honor their daughters by displaying special dolls and having tea parties. On Boys' Day, families wish their sons a good future by hanging a carp-shaped kite or windsock for each son outside their homes. The carp is a fish that symbolizes courage and endurance, two qualities Japanese hope their sons will have.

Notable Japanese Americans

Patsy Tekemoto Mink (1927–2002) Born in Paia, Hawaii, Mink was the first Japanese-American woman to become a lawyer in Hawaii. She became the first Nisei woman elected to the U.S. House of Representatives in 1954.

Noriyuki "Pat" Morita (1933–) Morita was born in Iselton, California. His parents were immigrant farm workers, and Morita and his family were interned at Manzanar during World War II. Morita gained popularity playing Arnold on the hit TV series *Happy Days* during the 1970s. In 1985, he was nominated for an Academy Award for Best Supporting Actor for his role in *The Karate Kid*.

Yoko Ono (1933–) An artist and musician born in Tokyo, Japan, Ono moved to the United States in 1951. She is best known as the wife and musical partner of John Lennon, who was a member of the rock band The Beatles.

Seiji Ozawa (1935–) Ozawa was born in Japan and became the first Japanese orchestra conductor to win widespread fame in the West. Leonard Bernstein, the legendary conductor of the New York Philharmonic, invited Ozawa to be the assistant conductor of the Philharmonic. Ozawa later served as conductor of the Toronto Symphony Orchestra, the San Francisco Symphony, and the Boston Symphony Orchestra.

Ellison Onizuka (1946–1986) Onizuka grew up in Hawaii and studied engineering at the University of Colorado. He was a test pilot and flight engineer for the U.S. Air Force, trained to be an astronaut in 1978, and was a mission specialist on the space shuttle *Discovery* in 1985. The first descendant of Japanese immigrants to fly in space, Onizuka was killed tragically onboard the space shuttle *Challenger* when it exploded shortly after takeoff on January 28, 1986.

RELIGION

Religion plays an important role in Japanese culture. The three main religions of Japan are Shinto (a religion that focuses on the emperor as a descendant of the sun goddess), Buddhism (a religion that believes people must become morally and mentally pure to be relieved of suffering), and Christianity (a Western religion that worships one God and His son, Jesus Christ).

A woman who immigrated to America in 1923 explained to her daughter how important religion is: "It is hard to become a good person by one's own strength. That's why we must draw from the strength of *kami-hotoke* (Buddhas and Shinto gods) for they are as different from humans as heaven is from earth. . . . A person who has religion will walk the road of Buddha's teachings: He will find happiness."

In Hawaii, many white leaders encouraged the Japanese to become Christian so they would have something in common with other residents of the islands. Reverend Takie Okamura, who became one of the most important Japanese Christians in Hawaii, expressed this opinion when he said:

> [The Nisei] ought to be brought up with the same belief as the rest of the Americans in the fatherhood of God and the brotherhood of man, if they are going to grow up and march forward shoulder to shoulder, clasping hands with their fellow Americans. Since we Christians worship the only God of heaven and earth and revere him as our spiritual Father, those of us who believe in God, therefore, have a common father.

When the Japanese came to America, they founded churches to serve their needs. Churches such as the Japanese Methodist Episcopal Church in San Francisco and the Seattle Buddhist Church met the spiritual needs of thousands of Japanese. Today, many Japanese continue to attend their own churches; others have joined mainstream denominations and worship with members of other ethnic and cultural groups.

Sushi, a traditional Japanese dish made of rice, spices, vinegar, and raw or cooked fish, has become a popular dish for many Americans, regardless of their ethnicity.

JAPANESE CONTRIBUTIONS TO AMERICAN CULTURE

Food

The Japanese have had an important influence on American culture. Japanese food is especially popular today. Foods such as sushi (a mixture of rice and raw or cooked seafood), tempura (deep-fried shrimp or vegetables), and teriyaki (meat or fish

Origami, a traditional Japanese art, involves folding colorful paper into intricate folds to create shapes, like flowers and plants, which are found in nature. Practicing traditional forms of Japanese art is one of the ways Japanese Americans preserve their heritage.

marinated in soy sauce) are enjoyed by millions of Americans. Edamame, or salted soybeans, are eaten as a snack and are sometimes called "Japanese peanuts." Soybeans are also processed to make miso soup and tofu (a soft, chewy, mild-tasting food that can be eaten with sauces and vegetables). Long noodles, such as udon or soba, are eaten with meats and vegetables in a sauce, or in bowls of soup.

Art

Japanese Americans also create beautiful works of art. Some use special pens to write in a special, fancy script called calligraphy.

Others create brush paintings, or fold pieces of paper into animal shapes in an art called *origami*. Japanese also consider flower arranging, called *ikebana*, to be an art, and they can create beautiful arrangements with carefully placed colors and shapes.

Japanese music sounds very different from Western music, because musicians use different instruments and a different system of note scales. A popular Japanese instrument is the *koto*, which is like a harp. Many Americans find koto music to be very soothing, and this style of music has grown in popularity over recent years.

Politics and Business

Along with the arts, the Japanese have influenced American society through politics and economics. Several Japanese Americans, particularly from Hawaii and California, have become important political figures in their states and in the federal government as well. It is no longer unusual for Japanese Americans to be part of the political process. Similarly, many successful companies, such as Sony, Honda, Minolta, and Nintendo were started in Japan and have become an enormous part of the American market. Japanese have also had an impact on America's entertainment culture, especially in baseball, which has long been a popular game among Japanese Americans.

The Japanese American of today bears little resemblance to the poor immigrant of 100 years ago, who faced devastating prejudice, racism, and economic hardship. In the words of Edwin O. Reischauer, former U.S. Ambassador to Japan, "It is remarkable what a large contribution to this country a relatively small number of Japanese have made despite great adversities."

Through hard work, perseverance, and a belief in the American way of life, the Japanese have become a vital part of the United States, and changed America's culture forever.

1639 Japanese rulers isolate the country from the rest of the world by passing laws forbidding anyone to enter or leave the country.

1853 Commodore Matthew Perry and his military force enter Japan and demand officials allow Japan to trade with other countries.

1868 Emperor Meiji allows Japanese citizens to emigrate. Immigration to Hawaii begins.

1882 The U.S. government passes the Chinese Exclusion Act, barring Chinese immigrants from the country. Japanese immigrants arrive to fill the gap and work as laborers on farms, railroads, and mines.

1886 Large-scale immigration of Japanese workers to Hawaii begins.

1888 The first Japanese laborers arrive in California.

1900 Hawaii becomes a U.S. territory. Plantation owners are no longer allowed to use contract labor.

1908 The "Gentlemen's Agreement" between the United States and Japan ends the immigration of Japanese laborers.

1921 The "Ladies' Agreement" between the United States and Japan ends the immigration of Japanese "picture brides" to the United States.

1922 The U.S. Supreme Court rules that Japanese immigrants cannot become U.S. citizens.

1924 The U.S. Immigration Act bans all immigration from Asia.

1941 Japan bombs the U.S. naval base at Pearl Harbor, Hawaii, on December 7. The United States declares war on Japan and enters World War II the next day.

1942–1945 Japanese residents of California, Oregon, and Washington are forced into internment camps.

1988 President George Bush officially apologizes to survivors of the internment camps, and Congress votes to pay each survivor $20,000.

Hoobler, Dorothy and Thomas. *The Japanese American Family Album.*
New York: Oxford University Press, 1996.

Hosokawa, Bill and Robert A. Wilson. *East to America: A History of the Japanese in the United States.* New York: William Morrow and Company, Inc., 1980.

Ichioka, Yuji. *The Issei: The World of the First Generation Japanese Immigrants.* New York: The Free Press, 1988.

"Japanese," *Encyclopedia of American Immigration.* Danbury, CT: Grolier Educational, 1999.

Kitano, Harry. *The Japanese Americans.* Philadelphia: Chelsea House Publishers, 1996.

Takaki, Ronald. *Issei and Nisei: The Settling of Japanese America.* Philadelphia: Chelsea House Publishers, 1994.

Wallner, Rosemary. *Japanese Immigrants 1850-1950.* Mankato, MN: Blue Earth Books, 2002.

Yancey, Diane. *Life in a Japanese American Internment Camp.* San Diego: Lucent Books, 1998.

FURTHER READING

FICTION

Blumberg, Rhoda. *Commodore Perry in the Land of the Shogun.* New York: Lothrop, Lee & Shepard, 1985.

Say, Allen. *Grandfather's Journey.* Boston: Houghton Mifflin, 1993.

NONFICTION

Alonso, Karen. *Korematsu v. United States: Japanese-American Internment Camps.* Springfield, NJ: Enslow Publishers, 1998.

Blumberg, Rhoda. *Shipwrecked! The True Adventures of a Japanese Boy.* New York: HarperCollins, 2000.

Chang, Juliana, ed. *Quiet Fire: A Historical Anthology of Asian American Poetry, 1892-1970.* Piscataway, NJ: Rutgers University Press, 1996.

Cooper, Michael L. *Fighting for Honor: Japanese Americans and World War II.* New York: Clarion Books, 2000.

Encyclopedia of American Immigration. Danbury, CT: Grolier Educational, 1999.

Houston, Jeanne Wakatsuki and James D. Houston. *Farewell to Manzanar.* Boston: Houghton Mifflin, 1973.

Leathers, Noel. *The Japanese in America.* Minneapolis: Lerner Publications, 1991.

Smith, Page. *Democracy on Trial.* New York: Simon & Schuster, 1995.

Tateishi, John. *And Justice for All.* New York: Random House, 1984.

Uchida, Yoshiko. *Desert Exile.* Seattle: University of Washington Press, 1982.

Angel Island Immigration Station
http://www.angelisland.org

Asian-Nation: The Landscape of Asian America
http://www.asian-nation.org

Immigration: The Japanese
http://library.thinkquest.org/20619/Japanese.html

Japanese American Citizens League
http://www.jacl.org

Japanese American History Archives
http://www.amacord.com/fillmore/museum/jt/jaha/jaha.html

Japanese American Internment Memorial
http://www.scu.edu/SCU/Programs/Diversity/memorial.html

National Japanese American History Society
http://www.njahs.org

The Japanese American Network
http://www.janet.org

Japanese American National Museum
369 East First Street
Los Angeles, CA 90012-3901

Japanese American World War II Library
16907 Brighton Avenue
Gardena, CA 90247

Manzanar National Historic Site
PO Box 426
Independence, CA 93526-0426

National Japanese American Historical Society
1684 Post Street
San Francisco, CA 94115-3604

INDEX

PICTURE CREDITS

ACKNOWLEDGMENTS

"My America" text on page 18 from *The Japanese American Family Album* by Dorothy & Thomas Hoobler, © 1996 by Dorothy & Thomas Hoobler. Used by permission of Oxford University Press, Inc.

CONTRIBUTORS

JOANNE MATTERN is the author of more than 125 books and articles for children. Her publications include contributions to *The Encyclopedia of American Immigration* (Grolier), *Coming to America* (Perfection Learning Corporation), and many other nonfiction works. Mrs. Mattern graduated from Hartwick College in Oneonta, New York, and worked as an editor at Morrow Junior Books and Troll Communications before becoming a full-time writer. She lives with her husband, two daughters, and several pets in the lower Hudson Valley of New York State.

DANIEL PATRICK MOYNIHAN is a former United States senator from New York. He is also the only person in American history to have served in the cabinets or subcabinets of four successive presidents—Kennedy, Johnson, Nixon, and Ford. Formerly a professor of government at Harvard University, he has written and edited many books.